Enhancement Edition

THE NEW TESTAMENT

THE GOSPEL OF JOHN

A Presentation of the Non-Synoptic Account of
Spiritual Truth That Extends Back to the Earliest
Point of Record

Robert E. Daley

The Larry Czerwonka Company, LLC
Hilo, Hawaiʻi

Copyright © 2015 by Robert E. Daley
All rights reserved.

No part of this publication may be reproduced, stored in or introduced into a retrieval system, or transmitted, in any form, or by any means (electronic, mechanical, photocopying, recording, or otherwise), without the prior permission of the publisher. Requests for permission should be directed to permissions@thelarryczerwonkacompany.com, or mailed to Permissions, The Larry Czerwonka Company, 1102 Apono Place, Hilo, Hawaii 96720.

First Edition — January 2016

This book is set in 14-point Garamond

Published by: The Larry Czerwonka Company, LLC
czerwonkapublishing.com

Printed in the United States of America

ISBN: 0692600280
ISBN-13: 978-0692600283

> **Quantity Sales Discounts**
> Larry Czerwonka Company titles are available at significant quantity discounts when purchased in bulk for client gifts, sales promotions, and premiums. Special editions, including books with corporate logos, customized covers, and letters from the company or CEO printed in the front matter, as well as excerpts of existing books, can also be created in large quantities for special needs. For details and discount information contact: sales@thelarryczerwonkacompany.com

All scriptures used in this work are taken from the
King James Version of the Scriptures.

BOOKS BY **ROBERT E. DALEY**

A Case for "Threes"
A Simple Plan . . . of Immense Complexity
Armour, Weapons, And Warfare
from Everlasting to Everlasting
Killer Sex
Life or Death, Heaven or Hell, You Choose!
Raptures and Resurrections
Short Tales
So . . . What Happens to the Package?
Study and Interpretation of The Scriptures Made Simple
Surviving Destruction as A Human Being
The Gospel of John
The Gospel of John (Red Edition)
The League of The Immortals
The New Testament - Pauline Revelation
The New Testament - Pauline Revelation Companion
"The World That Then Was . . ." & The Genesis That Now Is
What Color Are You?
What Makes A Christian Flaky?
What Really Happened to Judas Iscariot?
Who YOU Are in Christ . . . RIGHT NOW!

The Enhancement Series

    #1 Book of Ecclesiastes
    #2 Book of Daniel
    #3 Book of Romans
    #4 Book of Galatians
    #5 Book of Hebrews

The Deeper Things of God Series

    #1 The Personage of God
    #2 The Personage of Man
    #3 The Personage of Christ

Introduction

The sole purpose behind any enhancement is for simple clarity. There is no attempt whatsoever to present original manuscript alteration.

Within this small work, the King James Translation of the Bible is unchanged in its textual record. Some punctuation and translator added words may be altered, but the sole purpose behind that, is for a clearer understanding of divine thought by the reader.

Since this book is one of only four truly accurate accounts in existence, of the life of the man named Jesus Christ of Nazareth, while he is living on this planet named Earth and before his crucifixion, it is extremely important that the student of the Word of God have a clear cognizance of spiritual reality and truth. Jesus Christ is here and expressly exists, to definitively deal with the unrestricted operation of the Law of Sin situation, once and for all.

He is not here specifically to be a divine prophet . . . even though he *is* a genuine prophet of the One True God. He is not here specifically to be a teacher . . . even though he *is* an outstanding teacher concerning the issues of life. He is not here to specifically give us, and then leave us, a good example of how to live . . . even though the very example of how he did live *is* unprecedented. He is here to deal with Sin.

Failure to understand this reality, will lead to spiritual confusion, and religious insistence. Division among men will occur and souls shall be forever lost because of a lack of clarity.

THE GOSPEL OF JOHN

CHAPTER 1

1. *With*in *the Everlasting past, even before* **the beginning***, there* **was** *the Second Person of the Godhead entitled* **the Word.** *And the* **Word was with God** *the First Person of the Godhead***, and the Word was** *also* **God.**

2. **The same** *Personage* **was in the beginning with** *the Personage of* **God.**

3. **All** *created* **things were made by him; and without him was not any** *created* **thing made that was made.**

4. *Resident with***in him was** *Everlasting Spiritual* **Life;** **and the** *Everlasting Spiritual* **Life** *that was in him* **was the** *Given* **Light of men.**

5. **And the** *Given* **Light** *of men* **shineth** *within the midst of Spiritual* **darkness; and the** *Spiritual* **darkness comprehended it not.**

6. **There was a** *Human* **man sent** *forth* **from God, whose name was John.**

7. **The same** *man came forth to be* **a witness. To bear witness of the** *Given* **Light** *of men,* **that all** *other* **men through him might believe** *that Jesus of Nazareth is the Christ.*

8. **He was not that** *Given* **Light, but was sent to bear witness of that** *Given* **Light.**

9. **That** Given Light **was the true Light, which lighteth every** Human **man,** through his conscience, **that cometh into the world.**
10. **He was** resident with**in the world, and the world was** creatively **made by him, and the world knew him not.**
11. **He came unto his own** Hebrew people**, and his own** Hebrew people **received him not.**
12. **But as many** people **as received him** and what he has done, even unto today, **to them gave he** the creative power to actually **become the** very **sons of God, even to them that** simply **believe on his name.**
13. **Which were born, not** naturally **of blood, nor of the will of the flesh, nor of the** purposed **will of man, but** they are Spiritually Born **of God.**
14. **And the Word was** physically **made flesh, and dwelt among us, (and we beheld his** Express Image **glory, the glory as of the Only Begotten of the Heavenly Father,) full of grace and truth.**
15. And John did **bare witness of him, and cried, saying, This was he of whom I spake** unto you. **He that cometh after me is preferred before me; for he was** in existence long **before me.**
16. **And of his** glorious **fulness have all we received, and grace for grace.**
17. **For the** Mosaic **Law** that was needed for behavioral modification **was given** to the Hebrew people **by Moses, but** after his resurrection, unmerited **grace and** manifested **truth came by Jesus Christ.**

18.   *No man hath* actually *seen God* the Heavenly Father in the fullness of his glory *at any time. The Only Begotten Son, which is* manifest from with*in the bosom of the* Heavenly *Father, he hath declared him* unto us.
19.   *And this is the* true *record of John* the Baptist, *when the Jews sent priests and Levites from Jerusalem to ask* of *him, Who art thou?*
20.   *And he confessed* unto them, *and denied not; but confessed* unto them saying, *I am not the Christ.*
21.   *And they asked him* further, *What then? Art thou* the prophet *Elijah* that the Scriptures proclaim shall return? *And he saith, I am not. Art thou* then *That Prophet* that Moses spoke to us about that should come? *And he answered, No.*
22.   *Then said they unto him, Who art thou* then? *Tell* us *that we may* be able to *give an answer to them that sent us. What sayest thou of thyself?*
23.   *He said, I am the voice of one crying in the wilderness, "Make straight the way of the Lord", as said the prophet Isaiah.* (Isaiah 40:3-4)
24.   *And they which were sent* unto John *were of the Pharisees.*
25.   *And they asked him, and said unto him, Why baptizest thou* with water *then, if thou be not that Christ, nor* the prophet *Elijah, neither That Prophet* that Moses spoke to us about?
26.   *John answered them, saying, I baptize* thee *with water* only: *but* even now *there standeth one among you, whom ye know not.*
27.   *He it is, who coming* on the scene *after me is preferred before me, whose shoe's latchet I am not* even *worthy to unloose.*

28. *These things were done in* the village area of **Bethabara beyond Jordan, where John was baptizing.**
29. *The next day,* after the temptation of Jesus in the wilderness, **John seeth Jesus coming** back **unto him, and saith** prophetically, **Behold the Lamb of God, which taketh away the sin of the world!**
30. *This is he of whom I said* unto you, **After me cometh a man which is preferred before me; for he was before me.**
31. *And I* personally **knew him not. But that he should be made manifest to** the Nation of **Israel** as the promised Messiah, **therefore am I come baptizing with water.**
32. *And John* again **bare record, saying, I saw the** Holy **Spirit** of God **descending from heaven** appearing **like a dove, and it abode upon him.**
33. *And I* personally **knew him not. But he that sent me to baptize with water** only, who was the Personage of God, **the same said unto me, "Upon whom thou shalt see the** Holy **Spirit descending, and** then **remaining** upon **him, the same is he which** shall **baptizeth** thee **with the Holy Ghost** and with power."
34. *And I* personally *saw these things*, **and bare record that this** Jesus of Nazareth **is the Son of God.**
35. *Again the next day after* the first one, **John stood, and two of his disciples** stood with him.
36. *And looking upon Jesus as he walked, he saith* unto them, **Behold the Lamb of God!**
37. *And the two disciples heard him speak, and* they immediately left off following John and **they** then **followed Jesus.**

38. **Then Jesus turned** *himself about*, **and saw them following** *him*, **and saith unto them,** What seek ye? *And* **they said unto him, Rabbi (which is to say, being interpreted, Master,) where dwellest thou?**

39. **He saith unto them,** Come and see. **Then** *they* **came** *with him* **and saw where he dwelt, and** *they* **abode with him** *the rest of* **that day, for it was about the tenth hour.**

40. **One of the two** *men* **which heard John speak, and** *then* **followed him, was Andrew, Simon Peter's brother.**

41. **He first** *left where Jesus dwelt and* **findeth his own brother Simon, and saith unto him, We have found the** *promised* **Messiah, which is, being interpreted, the Christ.**

42. **And he** *persuaded Simon to come with him, and he* **brought him to Jesus. And when Jesus beheld him, he said** *under the Holy Spirit gifting of the Word of Knowledge*, Thou art Simon the son of Jonas. Thou shalt be called Cephas, which is by interpretation, A stone.

43. **The day following**, *which was the third day out of the wilderness*, **Jesus would** *purpose to* **go forth into Galilee** *because of a marriage feast invitation*, **and** *as he prepared to leave, he* **findeth Philip, and saith unto him,** Follow me.

44. **Now Philip was of Bethsaida** *in the north*, **the city of Andrew and Peter.**

45. **Philip** *then* **findeth Nathanael** *his friend*, **and saith unto him, We have found him, of whom Moses in the law, and the prophets** *confirming*, **did write** *about*; **Jesus of Nazareth, the son of Joseph.**

46. **And Nathanael said unto him,** *But* **can there any good thing come out of Nazareth? Philip saith unto him,** *Why don't you* **come and see?**

47. **Jesus saw Nathanael coming** *unto him*, **and saith of him** *by the Holy Spirit gifting of the Word of Knowledge*, Behold an Israelite indeed, in whom is no guile!

48. **Nathanael** *surprisingly* **saith unto him, whence knowest thou me? Jesus answered** *again, under the Holy Spirit gifting of the Word of Knowledge,* **and said unto him,** Before that Philip called thee, when thou wast under the fig tree, I saw thee.

49. **Nathanael**, *being astonished*, **answered and saith unto him, Rabbi, thou art** *truly* **the Son of God. Thou art the King of Israel.**

50. **Jesus answered and said unto him,** Because I said unto thee, I saw thee under the fig tree, believest thou *this*? Thou shalt see greater things than these.

51. **And he saith unto him,** Verily, verily, I say unto you, Hereafter ye shall see heaven open, and the angels of God ascending and descending upon the Son of man.

CHAPTER 2

1. **And** *also on* **the third day** *after the wilderness temptations,* **there was a marriage** *feast that had begun* **in** *the little city of* **Cana of Galilee. And the mother of Jesus was there** *at the marriage feast. When Jesus arrives in the city, he is reported to have five men with him that were not invited to the marriage. And when the governor of the marriage feast hears the report, he graciously extends an invitation to the men that have come with Jesus.*

2. **And** *so* **both Jesus was called, and his disciples, to the marriage.**

3. **And when** *at the marriage feast* **they wanted** *more* **wine, the mother of Jesus** *believing that he could remedy the situation* **saith unto him, They have no wine.**

4. **Jesus saith unto her,** **Woman, what have I to do with thee? Mine hour** *of public ministration* **is not yet come.**

5. **His mother** *knowing that her son could be of help,* **saith** *directly* **unto the servants, Whatsoever he saith unto you, do it.** *The eyes of the servants then shifted to Jesus in expectation.*

6. **And there were set there six water-pots of stone, after the manner of the purifying of the Jews, containing two or three firkins apiece,** *which is approximately twenty-seven gallons per water-pot.*

7. **Jesus saith unto them,** **Fill the water-pots with water.** **And they filled them up to the brim.**

8. **And he saith unto them,** **Draw out now, and bear** *it* **unto the governor of the feast.** **And they bare it.**

9.   When the ruler of the feast had tasted the water that was made *into* wine, and knew not *from whence it was,* (but the servants which drew the water knew,) the governor of the feast called the bridegroom *unto him.*

10.   And saith unto him, Every man at the beginning *of the feast* doth set forth *the* good wine *for his guests;* and when men have well drunk, then that *is served* which is worse. But thou hast kept the good wine until now.

11.   This beginning of *the Holy Spirit gifting of the Working of* Miracles did Jesus in *the city of* Cana of Galilee, and manifested forth his glory. And his First-Five disciples believed on him.

12.   After this he went down to Capernaum *on a ministerial scouting trip of relocation.* He, and his mother, and his brethren, and his First-Five disciples *all went.* And they continued there *for* not many days. *While they were there, Simon and Andrew and John left Jesus and returned to their fishing business with Zebedee. Philip and Nathanael departed from Jesus unto other unstated endeavors.*

13.   And the Jew's Passover *Celebration* was at hand, and *when it was time* Jesus went up to Jerusalem *in accordance to the requirements of the Law of Moses, all alone and without any disciples.*

14.   And *he* found *with*in the temple those that sold oxen and sheep and doves, and the changers of money sitting.

15.   And when he had made a scourge of small cords, he drove them all out of the temple *for the first time*, and the sheep, and the oxen. And *he* poured out the changers' money, and overthrew the tables.

16.   And said unto them that sold *the* doves, Take these things hence; make not my Father's house a house of merchandise.

17.   And *after that Jesus was risen from the dead,* his disciples remembered that it was written, "The zeal of thine house hath eaten me up." *(Psalms 69:9)*

18.   Then answered the Jews *at the time* and said unto him, What sign showest thou unto us, seeing that thou doest these things?

19.   Jesus answered and said unto them, Destroy this temple, and in three days I will raise it up.

20.   Then said the Jews, Forty and six years was this temple *of Herod* in the building *thereof*, and wilt thou rear it up *again* in *just* three days?

21.   But *the Jews did not understand that* he spake *to them* of the temple of his body.

22.   When therefore *that* he was risen from the dead, his disciples *again* remembered that he had said this unto them. And they *finally* believed the Scripture, and the word which Jesus had said.

23.   Now when *at that time* he was in Jerusalem at the Passover *Celebration*, in the *great* feast day, many believed in his name, when they saw the *Holy Spirit gifting of the Working of* Miracles which he did.

24. **But** *even then* **Jesus did not commit himself unto them, because** *through the working of the Holy Spirit gifting of the Word of Wisdom* **he knew all men,**
25. **And needed not that any should testify of** *the power of* **man. For he knew,** *by the Holy Spirit,* **what was resident with**in **man.**

CHAPTER 3

1. **There was a man of the** *sect of the* **Pharisees, named Nicodemus,** *who was* **a ruler of the Jews.**
2. **The same** *man, because of fear,* **came to Jesus** *secretly* **by night, and said unto him, Rabbi,** *within the Sanhedrin* **we know that thou art a teacher come from God: for no man can do these miracles that thou doest, except God be** *working* **with him.**
3. **Jesus answered and said unto him,** Verily, verily, I say unto thee *Nicodemus*, Except a man be *spiritually* Born-Again, he cannot *perceive, or see, or in anywise understand* the Kingdom of God.
4. **Nicodemus saith unto him, How can a** *grown* **man be born when he is** *already* **old? Can he enter the second time into his mother's womb, and be born** *once again?*
5. **Jesus answered,** Verily, verily, I say unto thee, Except a man be *physically* born of water *into this world,* and *then be born spiritually* of the Holy Spirit *of God, and pass from Spiritual Death unto Spiritual Life,* he cannot *legally* enter into the Kingdom of God.

6. *That which is* physically **born of the flesh is** *still only* **flesh** *and belongeth unto the Realm of the Natural.* **And that which is** *spiritually* **born of the** Holy **Spirit** *of God is* passed from Spiritual Death unto Spiritual Life, and belongeth unto the Realm of the **Spirit.**

7. **Marvel not that I said unto thee, Ye must be Born Again.**

8. **The wind,** *which ye cannot see,* **bloweth where it listeth, and thou hearest the sound thereof, but canst not tell** *from* **whence it cometh, and whither it goeth. So** *also* **is every one that is born of the** Holy **Spirit** *of God*.

9. **Nicodemus answered and said unto him, How can these things be?**

10. **Jesus answered and said unto him,** *Art thou a recognized* **master of** *spiritual issues within* **Israel, and** *yet* **knowest not** *ye of* **these things?**

11. **Verily, verily, I say unto thee, We** *readily* **speak of that** *which* **we do know, and testify** *of that* *which* **we have seen. And** *yet* **ye receive not our witness** *because ye know not of these spiritual things.*

12. **If I have told you** *of basic* **earthly things, and ye believe** *me* **not, how shall ye believe, if I** *shall* **tell you of** *much deeper* **heavenly things?**

13. **And** *I assure you that* **no man hath ascended up into the Heaven** *above*, **but he that came down from the Heaven, even the Son of man which,** *within the spirit,* **is in Heaven.**

14. **And as Moses lifted up the serpent in the wilderness** *so that the people who chose to gaze upon the serpent should be healed*, **even so must the Son of man be lifted up** *from the Earth*.

15. *That whosoever* that chooses to simply *believeth in him should not perish, but have Eternal Life.*

16. *For God so loved the* entire *world, that he gave his Only Begotten Son* as a sacrifice for Sin, *that whosoever believeth in him should not perish, but have Everlasting Life.*

17. *For God sent not his Son into the world* with the intent *to condemn the world, but that the* entire *world through him might be saved.*

18. *He that* simply *believeth on him is not condemned* unto damnation. *But he that believeth not is condemned already, because he hath not believed in the name of the Only Begotten Son of God.*

19. *And this is the condemnation* unto damnation, *that* the Given *Light is* personally *come into the world, and men loved* the *darkness rather than* the Given *Light, because their deeds were evil.*

20. *For every* single *one that doeth evil* literally *hateth the* Given *Light, neither* will he *cometh to the* Given *Light, lest his deeds should be reproved.*

21. *But he that doeth truth cometh to the* Given *Light, that his deeds may be made manifest that they are wrought in God.*

22. After these things, that Jesus had accomplished during the time that he had no disciples, then **came Jesus and his** second set of Faithful-Five **disciples into the land of Judea** for the purpose of ministerial training. **And there he tarried with them** for a time, **and baptized** men in water.

JOHN 3:31

23. **And John also was baptizing in** *the waters near to the town of* **Aenon** *which was* **near to Salim** *in the Region of Samaria,* **because there was much water there. And they came, and were baptized.**
24. **For John was not yet** *arrested and* **cast into prison.**
25. **Then there arose a question between some of John's disciples and the** *local* **Jews about purifying.**
26. **And they** *that were curious* **came unto John, and said unto him, Rabbi, he that was with thee beyond** *the* **Jordan, to whom thou** *began to* **bearest witness, behold, the same baptizeth** *with water down in Judea,* **and all men come unto him** *instead of thee.*
27. **John answered and said, A** *Human* **man can receive nothing, except it be given** *unto* **him from Heaven.**
28. **Ye yourselves bear me witness that I said** *that* **I am not the Christ, but that I am sent before him,** *to bear witness of him.*
29. *At any wedding feast,* **he that hath the bride is the bridegroom. But the friend of the bridegroom, which standeth** *at the door awaiting covenant confirmation,* **and** *then confirms that he* **heareth him, rejoiceth greatly because of the bridegroom's voice** *signifying fulfillment.* **This my joy therefore is fulfilled** *because of Heavenly confirmation.*
30. *From now on,* **he must increase, but I must decrease.**
31. **He that cometh from above is** *truly* **above all. He that is of the earth is earthly, and** *only* **speaketh of the earth. He that cometh from Heaven is above all** *and speaketh of spiritual things.*

32. And what*soever* he hath *personally* seen and heard, that *is what* he testifieth *of*. And no man receiveth his testimony.
33. He that hath received his testimony hath set to his seal *a bearing witness* that God is true.
34. For he whom God hath sent *from Heaven* speaketh the words of God. For God giveth not the *Holy* Spirit by measure unto him.
35. The Father *dearly* loveth the Son, and hath *authoritatively* given all things into his hand.
36. He that believeth on the *Only Begotten* Son *of* God hath Everlasting Life. And he that *chooseth to* believeth not *on* the Son *of God* shall not *ever* see Life; but *rather* the wrath of God *shall* abideth *up*on him.

CHAPTER 4

1. When therefore the Lord *Jesus* knew how the Pharisees had heard that *the Son of man named* Jesus made and baptized more disciples than John,
2. *(A*lthough Jesus himself baptized not, but his disciples *had been instructed in how to baptize,)*
3. He then left *the Region of* Judea, and departed again into *the Region of* Galilee.
4. And *in order to get there* he must needs go through *the Region of* Samaria.
5. Then cometh he to a city of *the Region of* Samaria, which is called Sychar, *which is* near to the parcel of ground that Jacob gave *unto* his son Joseph.

6.   Now Jacob's well was there. Jesus therefore, being wearied with his *ministerial* journey, sat thus on the well. And it was about the sixth hour *of the day.*

7.   There cometh, *at this unusual hour,* a woman of Samaria to draw water *for her household.* Jesus saith unto her, Please give me *something* to drink.

8.   (For his disciples were gone away unto the city *of Sychar* to buy meat.)

9.   Then saith the woman of Samaria unto him, How is it that thou, being a Jew, askest *a* drink of me, which am a woman of Samaria? For *it is well known that* the Jews have no dealings with the Samaritans.

10.   Jesus answered and said unto her, If thou *truly* knewest *of* the gift of God *that is extended unto thee*, and who it is that *actually* saith *unto thee,* Please give me *something* to drink; thou wouldest have *pleadingly* asked of him, and he would have given thee Living Water.

11.   The woman saith unto him, Sir, thou hast nothing to draw with, and the well is deep. From whence then hast thou *the capacity to give me* that Living Water?

12.   Art thou greater than our *fore*father Jacob, which *originally* gave us the well, and drank thereof himself, and *so did* his children, and *even* his cattle?

13.   Jesus answered and said unto her, Whosoever drinketh of this *natural* water shall thirst again.

14. *But whosoever shall* **drinketh of the** *Living* **Water that I shall give** *unto* **him shall never thirst; but the** *Living* **Water that I shall give** *unto* **him shall be in him a well of water** *continually* **springing up into Everlasting Life.**

15. **The woman saith unto him, Sir, give** *unto* **me this** *Living* **Water** *that ye speak of*, **that I thirst not, neither** *have to* **come hither to draw** *anymore*.

16. **Jesus saith unto her,** Go *forth*, call thy husband, and come hither.

17. **The woman** *sheepishly* **answered and said** *unto* **him, I have no husband. Jesus** *through the working of the Holy Spirit gifting of the Word of Knowledge* **said unto her, Thou hast well said, I have no husband.**

18. For thou hast had five husbands; and he whom thou now hast is not thy husband: in that saidest thou truly.

19. **The woman** *astonishingly* **saith unto him, Sir, I perceive that thou art a prophet** *of God*.

20. **Our** *fore*fathers *once* **worshipped in this mountain. And** *yet ye say,* **that in** *the City of* **Jerusalem is the place where men ought to worship.**

21. **Jesus saith unto her,** Woman, *please* believe me, the hour cometh, when ye shall neither in this mountain, nor yet at Jerusalem, worship the Heavenly **Father.**

22. Ye *continue to* worship ye know not what. We know *truly* what we worship; for salvation is *given* of the Jews.

23. But the hour cometh, and *even* now is, when the true worshippers *of God* shall worship the Heavenly Father in spirit and in truth. For the *Heavenly* Father seeketh such *faithful* to worship him.

24. God is a Spirit *Being*. And they that *will* worship him must worship him in spirit and in truth.

25. The woman saith unto him, I know that *the* Messiah cometh *soon,* which is called *the* Christ. When he is come, he will tell us *of* all things.

26. Jesus *soberly* saith unto her, I that speak unto thee am he.

27. And upon this *juncture* came his disciples *back from the city of Sychar,* and marveled that he talked with the woman *because the Jews have no dealings with the Samarians.* Yet no man said *unto her,* What seekest thou? or to *Jesus,* Why talkest thou with her?

28. The woman then left her waterpot *on the edge of the well,* and went her way into the city, and saith unto the men *of the city,*

29. Come, *and* see a man, which told me all things that ever I did. Is not this the Christ *that we have been waiting for?*

30. Then they went out of the city, and came unto him.

31. In the mean while his disciples prayed him, saying, Master, *please* eat *something.*

32. But he said unto them, I have meat to eat that ye know not of.

33. Therefore said the disciples one to another, *only perceiving the things that are natural,* Hath any man brought him aught to eat *while we were gone?*

34. **Jesus saith unto them,** My meat is to do the will of him that sent me, and to finish his work.

35. Say not ye, There are yet four months *left*, and then cometh *the* harvest? Behold, I say unto you, Lift up your eyes *unto spiritual things*, and look on the fields *even now*; for they are white already to harvest.

36. And he that *goeth forth to* reapeth, receiveth wages, and *he* gathereth fruit unto Life Eternal. That both he that *first* soweth and he that *later* reapeth may rejoice together.

37. And herein is that saying true, One *shall* soweth, and another *shall* reapeth.

38. I sent you to reap that whereon ye bestowed no labour *in sowing*. Other men labored *in sowing*, and ye are entered into, *and partake of,* their labours.

39. **And many of the Samaritans of that city believed on him for the saying of the woman, which testified, He told me all that ever I did.**

40. **So when the Samaritans were come unto him, they besought him that he would tarry with them, and he** *agreed and* **abode there** *for* **two days.**

41. **And many more believed** *while he was there* **because of his own word** *that he spoke.*

42. **And** *they* **said unto the woman, Now we believe,** *but* **not because of thy saying.** *Rather,* **for** *because* **we have heard him** *for* **ourselves, and** *now we* **know that this is indeed the Christ, the Saviour of the world.**

43. **Now after** *the* **two days** *had passed* **he departed thence, and went into** *the Region of* **Galilee.**

44. *For* **Jesus himself testified, that a prophet hath no honour in his own country.**

45. *Then,* **when he was come into** *the Region of* **Galilee, the Galileans** *readily* **received him, having seen all** *of* **the things that he did at Jerusalem at the feast** *of the Passover.* **For they also went unto the feast** *according to the Law of Moses.*

46. *So* **Jesus came again into** *the city of* **Cana** *in the Region* **of Galilee, where he** *had* **made the water** *into* **wine. And there was a certain nobleman, whose son was sick** *down* **at** *the city of* **Capernaum.**

47. **When he** *had* **heard that Jesus was come out of** *the Region of* **Judea** *and* **into the Galilee** *Region,* **he** *purposed and* **went unto him and besought him that he would come down** *to Capernaum,* **and heal his son: for he was at the point of death.**

48. **Then said Jesus unto him,** **Except ye** *all* **see signs and wonders, ye will not believe.**

49. **The nobleman** *through anguish* **saith unto him, Sir,** *please* **come down ere my child die.**

50. **Jesus** *exercising the Holy Spirit gifting of the Working of Miracles,* **saith unto him,** **Go thy way;** *for* **thy son liveth.** **And the man** *then* **believed the word that Jesus had spoken unto him, and he went his way.**

51. **And as he was now going** *back* **down** *to the city of Capernaum,* **his servants** *who were coming to him* **met him, and** *happily* **told him, saying, Thy son liveth.**

52. **Then inquired he of them** *concerning* **the hour when he began to amend. And they said unto him,** *It was* **yesterday at the seventh hour** *that* **the fever left him.**

53.   So the father knew that it was at the same hour, in the which Jesus *had* said unto him, Thy son liveth. *And himself believed, and his whole house.*
54.   This is again the second miracle that Jesus did *while at the city of Cana*, when he was come out of *the Region of* Judea *and* into Galilee.

Chapter 5

1.   After this there was a*nother* feast *which was celebrated* of the Jews; and Jesus went up to Jerusalem *in accordance to the Law of Moses.*
2.   Now there is at Jerusalem, by the sheep market, a pool which is called in the Hebrew tongue Bethesda, having five porches.
3.   In these *porches* lay a great multitude of impotent folk. Of blind, *and* halt, *and physically* withered, *who were anxiously* waiting for the moving of the water.
4.   For an angel *from Heaven* went down at a certain season into the pool, and troubled the water. Whosoever then first, after the troubling of the water, stepped into *the pool* was made whole of whatsoever disease he had.
5.   And a certain man was there, which had an infirmity *for* thirty and eight years *now*.

6.   **When Jesus saw him lie, and** *through the working of the Holy Spirit gifting of the Word of Knowledge,* **knew that he had been now a long time in that case,** he *had compassion on him and* **saith unto him,** Wilt thou be made whole?

7.   **The impotent man** *hesitantly* **answered him, Sir, I have no man** *with me,* **when the water is troubled, to put me into the pool. But while I am coming** *to get into the water,* **another steppeth down before me.**

8.   **Jesus** *operating through the working of the Holy Spirit gift of Healing* **saith unto him,** Rise, take up thy bed, and walk.

9.   **And immediately the man was made whole, and** *he* **took up his bed, and walked. And on the same day was the Sabbath** *of Commandment.*

10.   **The Jews** *around the sheep market area* **therefore said unto him that was cured, It is the Sabbath day. It is not lawful for thee to carry thy bed.**

11.   **He answered** *unto* **them, He that made me whole** *from my infirmity,* **the same said unto me, Take up thy bed, and walk.**

12.   **Then asked they** *of* **him,** *Show us* **what man is that, which said unto thee, Take up thy bed and walk.**

13.   **And he that was healed** *looked around and* **wist not who it was: for Jesus had conveyed himself away, a multitude being in that place.**

14.   **Afterward Jesus findeth him in the temple,** *and approached him* **and said unto him,** Behold, thou art made whole *of thine infirmity*: sin no more, lest a worse thing come unto thee.

JOHN 5:15

15. *The man departed* from the temple, *and told the Jews that it was Jesus, which had made him whole.*

16. *And therefore did the Jews* seek him out, and began to *persecute Jesus, and sought to* bring him to the religious rulers to *slay him, because he had done these things on the Sabbath Day* of Commandment.

17. *But Jesus answered* unto *them,* *My Father in Heaven* worketh hitherto, and I work.

18. *Therefore the Jews sought* even *the more to kill him, because he not only had broken the Sabbath* Day in their opinion, *but said also that God in Heaven was his Father, making himself equal with God.*

19. *Then answered Jesus* their protests *and said unto them,* Verily, verily, I say unto you, The Son of man can do nothing of himself, but only what he seeth the Heavenly Father do. For what things soever he doeth, these also doeth the Son likewise.

20. For the Heavenly Father loveth the Son, and showeth him all things that himself doeth. And he will show unto him greater works than these that ye see, that ye may marvel.

21. For as the Heavenly Father raiseth up the dead, and quickeneth them back to life; even so the Son quickeneth whom he will.

22. For the Heavenly Father hath chosen to judgeth no man, but hath instead committed all judgment unto the Son.

23. *So* **that all men should honour the Son, even as they honour the** *Heavenly* **Father. He that honoureth not the Son** *of God* **honoureth not the** *Heavenly* **Father which hath sent him.**

24. **Verily, verily, I say unto you, He that** *truly* **heareth my word, and believeth on him that sent me, hath Everlasting** *Spiritual* **Life, and shall not come into condemnation; but is passed from** *Spiritual* **Death unto** *Spiritual* **Life.**

25. **Verily, verily, I say unto you, The hour is coming, and now is, when the** *Spiritually* **Dead shall hear the voice of the Son of God and they that hear** *and believe* **shall** *Spiritually* **Live.**

26. **For as the** *Heavenly* **Father hath** *Eternal Spiritual* **Life in himself; so hath he given to the Son to have** *Eternal Spiritual* **Life in himself.**

27. **And hath given him** *the* **authority to execute** *final* **judgment also, because he is the Son of man.**

28. **Marvel not at this. For the hour is coming, in the which all that are in the graves shall hear his voice,**

29. **And** *they* **shall** *all* **come forth** *from the graves.* **They that have done good** *and believeth on him whom the Heavenly Father hath sent,* **unto the resurrection of** *Eternal Spiritual* **Life. And they that have done evil** *and do not believeth on him whom the Heavenly Father hath sent,* **unto the resurrection of Damnation.**

30. *Even as the Son of man,* **I can of mine own self do nothing. As I hear, I** *thus* **judge. And my judgment is** *going to be* **just; because I seek not mine own will, but the will of the** *Heavenly* **Father which hath sent me.**

31. *If I, as a man,* **bear witness of myself, my witness is not true.**

32. **There is another that beareth witness of me** *which is the written Spirit of Truth;* **and I know that the witness which he** *has declared and* **witnesseth of me is true.**

33. **Ye sent unto John** *to inquire of Scriptural declaration,* **and he bare witness unto the truth** *of what he heard and saw.*

34. **But I receive not** *confirming* **testimony from** *any* **man,** *even John:* **but these things I say, that ye might** *ultimately* **be saved.**

35. **He was a burning and a shining light** *of prophetical witness:* **and ye were willing for a season to rejoice in his light.**

36. **But I have a greater witness than that of John. For the** *very* **works which the** *Heavenly* **Father hath given me to finish,** *even* **the** *exact* **same works that I do, bear witness of me, that the** *Heavenly* **Father hath sent me.**

37. **And the** *Heavenly* **Father himself, which hath sent me, hath borne witness of me** *both verbally and Scripturally.* **But ye have neither heard his voice at any time, nor seen his** *likeness* **shape.**

38. **And ye have not his word abiding in you. For whom he hath sent, him ye believe not.**

39. **Search the Scriptures; for in them ye think ye have Eternal** *Spiritual* **Life. And they are they which testify of me.**

40. **And ye will not come** *unto* **me, that ye might have** *the Light of* **Life** *because your deeds are evil.*

41. **I receive not honour from** *natural* **man.**

42. *But I know of you, that ye have not the love of God in you.*

43. *I am come in my* Heavenly *Father's name, and ye receive me not. If another* man *shall come in his own name, him ye will receive.*

44. *How can ye* ever *believe, which receive honour one of another* among men, *and seek not the honour that cometh from God only?*

45. *Do not think that I will accuse you to the* Heavenly *Father. There is* that *one that* already *accuseth you, even Moses, in whom you trust.*

46. *For had ye* truly *believed* what *Moses* had to say, *ye would have believed me: for he* originally *wrote of me.*

47. *But if ye believe not his writings, how shall ye believe my words?*

Chapter 6

1. *An extended period of time* **after these things Jesus went over the Sea of Galilee, which is** *also known of as* **the Sea of Tiberius.**

2. **And a great multitude** *of people* **followed him, because they saw the miracles which he did on them that were diseased** *and they desired to receive from him.*

3. **And Jesus**, *when he arrived on the other side of the sea,* **went up into a mountain, and there he sat with his disciples.**

4. **And the Passover** *Celebration,* **a feast of the Jews, was nigh** *again.*

5. **When Jesus then**, *in the process of time,* **lifted up his eyes, and saw a great company** *of followers* **coming unto him, he saith unto Philip,** Whence shall we buy bread, that these may *be able to* eat?
6. **And this he said to prove him** *concerning the ministerial instructions that he had been giving unto his disciples;* **for he himself knew what he would do.**
7. **Philip** *still totally focusing on the natural* **answered him, Two hundred pennyworth of bread is not sufficient for them, that every one of them may take a little.**
8. **One of his disciples, Andrew,** *who was* **Simon Peter's brother,** *remembering some of the instructions that Jesus had been giving* **saith unto him,**
9. **There is a** *young* **lad here, which hath five barley loaves, and two small fishes. But what are they among so many**, *Andrew being overwhelmed by the size of the multitude that gathered*?
10. **And Jesus said** *unto them,* Make the men to sit down. **Now there was** *fortunately* **much grass in the place. So** *accounting for* **the men** *only, they* **sat down, in number about five thousand.**
11. **And Jesus took the** *five* **loaves; and when he had given thanks***giving unto God, and utilizing the Holy Spirit gifting of the Working of Miracles,* **he distributed the loaves to the disciples, and the disciples** *distributed the loaves un***to them that were set down; and likewise** *also* **of the** *small* **fishes as much as they would** *desire to eat.*
12. **When they were** *finally* **filled, he said unto his disciples,** Gather up *carefully* the fragments *of the loaves and the fishes* that remain, that nothing *shall* be lost.

JOHN 6:19

13.   Therefore they gathered them together, and filled *up* twelve baskets with the fragments *only*, of the five barley loaves *and the small fishes*, which remained over and above unto *all of* them that had eaten.

14.   Then those men *that were gathered*, when they had seen the miracle that Jesus did, said, This is of a truth That Prophet that should come into the world.

15.   When Jesus therefore *by both the Holy Spirit gifting of the Word of Wisdom and the Word of Knowledge* perceived that they would come and take him by force, to make *of* him a king, he departed again into a mountain *all by* himself, alone.

16.   And when *the evening time* was now come, his disciples went down *from the mountain side* unto the seashore,

17.   And *they* entered into a ship, and went over the *northern part of the* sea toward Capernaum. And it was now dark, and Jesus was not come *un*to them.

18.   And the sea arose by reason of a great wind that blew.

19.   So *they struggled with the rowing of the ship, and* when they had rowed about *halfway across the upper portion of the sea, which was* five and twenty or thirty furlongs, *or approximately four miles*, they *suddenly* see Jesus walking on the sea, and drawing nigh unto the ship. And they were *naturally* afraid.

JOHN 6:20

20.   **But** as he drew nigh, **he saith unto them,** It is only I, be not afraid.

21.   **Then they willingly received him into the ship. And** Jesus utilizing the Holy Spirit gifting of the Working of Miracles, caused that **immediately the ship was at the land whither they went.**

22.   **The day following, when the** multitude of **people, which stood on the other side of the sea** near to Tiberius, **saw that there was none other boat there, save** for **that one whereinto his disciples were entered; and** they knew **that Jesus went not with his disciples into the boat, but that his disciples were gone away alone** and without him;

23.   **(Howbeit there came other boats** in the interim **from Tiberius nigh unto the place where they did eat** of the **bread** and the fishes, **after that the Lord had given thanks :)**

24.   **When** many of **the people therefore saw that Jesus was not** anywhere there**about,** and **neither** were **his disciples, they also took shipping, and came to Capernaum, seeking for Jesus** to perform another miracle and feed them again.

25.   **And when they had** finally **found him on the other side of the sea** within the synagogue in Capernaum, **they said unto him, Rabbi, when camest thou hither?**

26.   **Jesus answered them and said,** Verily, verily, I say unto you, Ye seek me, not because ye saw the miracles and ye did believe, but only because ye did eat of the loaves and the fishes, and were filled.

JOHN 6:36

27. *I counsel thee to* **labour not for the** *physical* **meat which perisheth, but for that** *spiritual* **meat which endureth unto Everlasting Life, which the Son of man shall give unto you. For him hath God the Father sealed** *unto this purpose.*

28. Then said they unto him, What shall we do *then***, that we might work the works of God?**

29. Jesus answered and said unto them, *This is what* **the work of God** *is all about***, that ye believe on him whom he hath sent.**

30. They said therefore unto him, What *kind of a* **sign showest thou then** *unto us***, that we may see** *with our eyes***, and** *then* **believe thee? What doest thou work?**

31. Our fathers did eat manna *when they were* **in the desert; as it is written, "He gave** *unto* **them bread from Heaven to eat."** *(Exodus 16:15)*

32. Then Jesus said unto them, *Verily, verily, I say unto you,* **Moses gave you not that** *natural* **bread from Heaven. But my** *Heavenly* **Father giveth you the true** *Spiritual* **Bread** *that is* **from Heaven.**

33. *For the Spiritual* **Bread of God is** *truly* **he which cometh down from Heaven, and giveth** *Everlasting* **Life unto the world.**

34. Then said they unto him, Lord, evermore give *unto* **us this** *Spiritual* **Bread.**

35. And Jesus said unto them, I *myself* **am the** *Spiritual* **Bread of** *Everlasting* **Life. He that cometh** *unto me and believeth***, shall never hunger; and he that** *truly* **believeth on me shall never thirst** *again.*

36. But I said unto you, That ye also have *personally* **seen me, and** *yet ye* **believe not** *on me.*

37. *All* of the children *that the* Heavenly *Father giveth* unto *me shall come* unto *me; and him that cometh* unto *me I will in no wise* ever *cast out.*

38. *For I* personally *came down from Heaven, not to do mine own will, but the will of him that sent me.*

39. *And this is the* Heavenly *Father's will which hath sent me, that of all* of the children *which he hath given* unto *me I should lose nothing, but should raise him up again at the last day.*

40. *And this is the will of him that sent me, that every one which seeth the Son, and* particularly they which *believeth on him, may have Everlasting Life. And I will* then *raise him up at the last day.*

41. **The Jews** of the multitude **then murmured at him, because he said, I am the** Spiritual **Bread which came down from Heaven.**

42. **And they said** among themselves**, Is not this Jesus, the son of Joseph** of Nazareth**, whose father and mother we** actually **know? How is it then that he saith, I** personally **came down from Heaven?**

43. **Jesus therefore answered and said unto them,** *Murmur not among yourselves.*

44. *No man can come* unto *me, except the* Heavenly *Father which hath sent me draw him* by the power of the Holy Spirit. *And I will* then *raise him up at the last day.*

45. *It is written in the prophets, "And they shall be all taught of God."* (Isaiah 54:13) *Every man therefore that hath heard* from the Holy Spirit*, and hath learned of the* Heavenly *Father, cometh unto me.*

46. Not that any man hath seen the Heavenly Father in all of his glory, save he which is of God. He alone hath seen the loving Heavenly Father because he came forth from his bosom.

47. Verily, verily, I say unto you, He that chooseth to believeth on me hath Everlasting Life.

48. I am that Spiritual Bread of Everlasting Life.

49. Your fathers did eat of the natural manna in the wilderness, and they are now dead.

50. This that I speak to you concerning, is the Spiritual Bread of God which cometh down from Heaven, that a man may eat thereof, and not ever die.

51. I am the Living Spiritual Bread which personally came down from Heaven. If any man eat of this Spiritual Bread of God, he shall live forever. And the Spiritual Bread that I will give unto Humanity is my flesh, for the Word of God was indeed made flesh, which I will give for the Spiritual Life of the world.

52. The Jews therefore strove among themselves and reasoned, saying, How can this man give unto us his actual flesh to eat?

53. Then Jesus said unto them, Verily, verily, I say unto you, Except ye eat of the flesh of the son of man, and drink of his blood, ye have no life in you.

54. Whoso eateth of my flesh which is the Living Word of God, and drinketh of my blood which is the very Force of Life, hath Eternal Spiritual Life. And I will then raise him up at the last day.

55. For my flesh is spiritual meat indeed, and my blood is spiritual drink indeed.

JOHN 6:56

56. *He that eateth* of *my flesh* which is the Living Word of God, *and drinketh* of *my blood* which is the very Force of Life, *dwelleth in me, and I in him.*

57. *As the Living* Heavenly *Father hath sent me* to the Earth, *and as I live by the* power of the Heavenly *Father; so he that eateth* of *me, even he shall live by* the power that dwelleth in *me.*

58. *This is that* Spiritual *Bread which came down from Heaven. Not as your fathers did eat* the natural *manna, and are* now *dead. He that eateth of this* Spiritual *Bread shall live for ever*more.

59. *These things said he* when he was *in the synagogue, as he taught in Capernaum.*

60. *Many therefore of his disciples, when they had heard this, said, This is a hard saying; who can hear it?*

61. *When Jesus knew* with*in himself,* because of the working of the Holy Spirit gift of the Word of Knowledge, *that his* own twelve *disciples murmured at it, he said unto them,* Doth this offend you also?

62. *What and if ye shall see the Son of man ascend up* to *where he was before?* What then?

63. *It is the* Holy *Spirit that quickeneth* and make alive, *the flesh* verily *profiteth nothing. The* very *words that I speak unto you,* in reality *they are* words of *spirit, and they are* words of *Life.*

64. *But there are* even now *some of you that believe not.* For Jesus knew, by the working of the Holy Spirit gifting of the Word of Knowledge, *from the beginning* of the end, *who they were* among them *that believed not, and* additionally *who should betray him.*

65.   **And he said,** Therefore said I unto you the truth, **that no man can come unto me, except it were given unto him of my Father.**

66.   *And* **from that time** *forth* **many of his disciples went back, and walked no more with him.**

67.   **Then said Jesus unto the twelve,** Will ye also go away?

68.   **Then Simon Peter answered him, Lord, to whom shall we go? Thou** *alone* **hast the words of Eternal Life.**

69.   **And we believe and are sure that thou art that Christ, the Son of the living God.**

70.   **Jesus answered them,** Have not I *personally* chosen you twelve, and *yet* one of you is a devil.

71.   **He spake** *of course* **of Judas Iscariot the son of Simon. For he it was that should** *ultimately* **betray him, being one of the twelve.**

Chapter 7

1.   **After these things Jesus walked** *with***in** *the Region of* **Galilee** *where his ministerial headquarters were.* **For** *the time* **he would not walk** *in Judea,* **within Jewry, because the Jews sought to kill him.**

2.   **Now the Jews' Feast of Tabernacles was** *nigh* **at hand.**

3.   **His** *family* **brethren therefore said unto him** *mockingly,* **Depart hence, and go into** *the Region of* **Judea, that** *all of* **thy** *other* **disciples also may see the works that thou doest.**

4. **For there is no man that doeth anything in secret, and he himself** *really* **seeketh to be known openly. If thou do**est **these** *marvelous* **things, show thyself to the world.**
5. **For neither did his** *own family* **brethren believe in him.**
6. **Then Jesus said unto them,** *My time is not yet come. But your time is always ready.*
7. *The world cannot hate you* because you are of the world. *But me it hateth, because I testify of it, that the works thereof are evil.*
8. *Go ye up unto this feast,* even as the Law of Moses requires. *I go not up yet unto this feast; for my time is not yet full come.*
9. *And* **when he had said these words unto them, he abode still in Galilee.**
10. **But when his** *own family* **brethren were gone up, then went he also up unto the feast** under the leading of the Holy Spirit, **not openly, but as it were in secret.**
11. **Then the Jews** *of Judea* **sought him at the feast, and said, Where is he?**
12. **And there was much murmuring among the people concerning him. For some** *people* **said, He is a good man:** *and* **others said, Nay; but he deceiveth the people.**
13. **Howbeit no man spake openly of him for fear of the** *religious* **Jews** *which openly hated him and sought to kill him.*
14. **Now about the midst of the feast**, at the leading of the Holy Spirit, **Jesus went up into the temple, and taught.**

15. **And the** *local* **Jews marveled, saying, How knoweth this man** *his* **letters, having never** *formally* **learned?**

16. **Jesus answered them, and said,** My doctrine is not *actually* mine, but *rather it is* his that sent me.

17. If any man will *purpose to* do his will, he shall know of the doctrine, whether it *really* be of God, or whether I speak of myself.

18. He that speaketh of himself *always* seeketh his own glory. But he that seeketh his glory that *originally* sent him, the same is true, and no unrighteousness is in him.

19. Did not Moses give you the Law? And yet none of you keepeth the law. *So* why go ye about to kill me?

20. **The** *religious* **people** *who were angry with him* **answered and said, Thou hast a devil. Who** *is it that* **goeth about to kill thee?**

21. **Jesus answered and said unto them,** I have done *only* one work, and ye all marvel.

22. Moses therefore gave unto you circumcision. (Not because it is *actually* of Moses, but *it was passed down* of the fathers.) And ye on the Sabbath Day *of Commandment do* circumcise a man.

23. If *therefore* a man on the Sabbath Day *of Commandment* receive circumcision, that the Law of Moses should not be broken; are ye *so* angry at me, because I have made a man every whit *physically* whole on the *same* Sabbath Day *of Commandment?*

24. Judge not according to the appearance *of the situation*, but judge righteous judgment.

25. Then said some of them of Jerusalem *who were not angry with him*, **Is not this he, whom they** *are* **seeking** *to* **kill?**
26. **But, lo, he speaketh boldly, and** *yet* **they** *publically* **say nothing unto him. Do the rulers** *really* **know indeed that this is the very Christ?**
27. **Howbeit we know this man** *from* **whence he is. But when Christ cometh, no man** *shall* **knoweth whence he is.**
28. **Then cried Jesus in the temple as he taught, saying,** Ye both know me, and ye know *from* whence I am. And I am not come *here* of myself, but he that sent me is true, whom ye know not.
29. But I know him; for I am *come* from him, and he *is the one who* hath sent me.
30. **Then they sought to take him** *again*. **But no man laid** *his* **hands** *up***on him, because his hour was not yet come.**
31. **And many of the** *local* **people believed on him, and said, When** *the* **Christ cometh, will he do more miracles than these which this man hath done?**
32. **The Pharisees** *then* **heard that the people murmured such things concerning him. And** *so* **the Pharisees and the chief priests** *conspired together, and* **sent** *the* **officers** *of the temple* **to take** *hold of* **him.**
33. **Then said Jesus unto them,** Yet *only* a little while am I with you, and then I go *back* unto him that sent me.
34. Ye shall seek *after* me, and shall not find me. And where I am, thither ye cannot come.

35. Then said the *local* **Jews among themselves, Whither will he go, that we shall not** *be able to* **find him? Will he go unto the dispersed** *Jews* **among the Gentiles, and teach the Gentiles** *also?*

36. **What manner of saying is this that he said, Ye shall seek** *after* **me, and shall not find me? And, where I am thither ye cannot come.**

37. **In the last day, that Great Day of the feast, Jesus stood** *in the midst* **and cried, saying,** **If any man thirst, let him come unto me, and drink.**

38. **He that believeth on me, as the Scripture hath said, out of his belly shall flow rivers of Living Water.**

39. **(But this spake he of the** *Holy* **Spirit, which they that believe on him should receive. For the Holy Ghost was not yet given, because that Jesus was not yet** *resurrected from the dead and* **glorified.)**

40. **Many of the** *local* **people therefore, when they heard this saying, said, Of a truth, this is That Prophet** *that Moses spake of*.

41. **Others said, This is** *indeed* **the Christ. But some said, Shall** *the* **Christ come out of** *the* **Region of Galilee?**

42. **Hath not the Scriptures said that** *the* **Christ cometh of the seed of David, and out of the town of Bethlehem, where David was?**

43. **So there was a division among the people because of him.**

44. **And some of them would have taken him** *and had him arrested;* **but no man laid** *their* **hands on him.**

45.   Then came the officers *of the temple back un***to the chief priests and Pharisees. And they said unto them, Why have ye not brought him** *to us?*
46.   **The officers answered** *them,* **Never** *any* **man spake like this man.**
47.   **Then answered** *unto* **them the Pharisees, Are ye also deceived?**
48.   **Have any of the rulers** *that you know of,* **or** *men* **of the Pharisees believed on him?**
49.   **But this people who knoweth not the law are cursed.**
50.   **Nicodemus saith unto them, (he that came to Jesus by night,** *actually* **being one of them.)**
51.   **Doth our law** *pre-***judge any man, before it hear***eth* **him, and know***eth* **what he doeth?**
52.   **They answered and said unto him, Art thou also** *come out* **of Galilee? Search, and look: for out of** *the Region of* **Galilee ariseth no prophet.**
53.   **And** *when they had concluded their discussion,* **every man went unto his own house.**

CHAPTER 8

1.   *Jesus then* **went unto the mount of Olives.**
2.   **And early in the morning he came** *once* **again into the temple, and all** *of* **the people came unto him** *to hear him.* **And he sat down, and taught them.**
3.   **And the scribes and** *the* **Pharisees brought unto him a woman taken in adultery** *that they might trap him in his words.* **And when they had set her in the midst** *of those that he was teaching,*

4. **They say unto him, Master, this woman was taken in adultry, in the very act.**

5. **Now Moses, in the law, commanded us that such** *a transgressor* **should be stoned** *to death*; **but what sayest thou?**

6. **This they said, tempting him, that they might have** *something* **to accuse him** *of*. **But Jesus stooped down, and with his finger wrote on the ground, as though he heard them not,** *fulfilling the saying of Jeremiah the prophet.* *(Jeremiah 17:13)*

7. **So when they continued asking him, he lifted up himself, and said unto them,** He that is without *any* sin among you, let him first cast a stone at her.

8. **And again he stooped down, and wrote on the ground.**

9. **And they which heard it, being convicted by their own conscience, went out one by one, beginning at the eldest, even unto the last. And Jesus was left alone, and the woman standing in the midst** *of the people that he was teaching.*

10. **When Jesus had** *finished his writing,* **he lifted up himself, and saw none** *of the accusers there,* **but the woman** *only,* **and he said unto her,** Woman, where are those thine accusers? Hath no man condemned thee?

11. *And* **she said, No man, Lord. And Jesus said unto her,** Neither do I condemn thee: go *your way* and sin no more.

JOHN 8:12

12. *Then spake Jesus again unto them, saying,* I am the Given Light of the world. He that followeth me shall not walk in darkness, but shall have the light of Everlasting Spiritual Life.

13. **The Pharisees therefore said unto him, Thou** only **bearest record of thyself;** and so **thy record is not true.**

14. But **Jesus answered and said unto them, Though I** do **bear record of myself, yet my record is true. For I know** from **whence I came and** to **whither I go; but ye cannot tell** either **whence I come, and whither I go.**

15. Ye judge men after the flesh; I judge no man at this time.

16. And yet if I judge, my judgment is true: for I am not alone, but I and the Heavenly Father that sent me.

17. It is also written in your law, that the testimony of two men is true.

18. I am one that bear witness of myself, and the Heavenly Father that sent me is the second that also beareth witness of me through the Scriptures.

19. **Then said they unto him, Where is thy Father? Jesus answered,** Ye neither know me, nor my Heavenly Father. If ye had known me, ye should have known my Heavenly Father also.

20. **These words spake Jesus** when he was **in the treasury, as he taught in the temple. And no man laid** their **hands on him; for his hour was not yet come.**

21. **Then said Jesus again unto them,** *I go my way, and ye shall seek me, and shall die in your sins. Whither I go, ye cannot come.*

22. **Then said the Jews, Will he kill himself? Because he saith,** *Whither I go, ye cannot come.*

23. **And he said unto them,** *Ye are from* this world *beneath;* and *I am from* the Heaven *above. Ye are of this world* and the system of this world*; and I am not of this world.*

24. *I said therefore unto you, that ye shall die in your sins. For if ye believe not that I Am, ye shall die in your sins.*

25. **Then said they unto him, Who art thou? And Jesus saith unto them,** *Even the same that I said unto you from the beginning.*

26. *I have many things to say and to judge of you* of my own Human self*. But he that sent me is true; and I* choose to *speak to the world* only *those things which I have heard of him.*

27. **They understood not that he spake to them of the** Heavenly **Father.**

28. **Then said Jesus unto them,** *When ye have lifted up the Son of man* from off of the Earth*, then shall ye know that I Am, and that I do nothing of myself; but as my* Heavenly *Father hath taught me* by the Holy Spirit in his word*, I speak these things.*

29. *And he that sent me is with me. The* Heavenly *Father hath not left me alone; for I do always those things that please him.*

30. **As he spake these words** in the temple**, many believed on him.**

JOHN 8:31

31.   Then said Jesus to those Jews *specifically* which believed on him, If ye continue in my word, then are ye my disciples indeed;
32.   And ye shall know the truth, and the truth shall make you free.
33.   They answered him, We be *of* Abraham's seed, and were never in bondage to any man. How sayest thou, Ye shall be made free?
34.   Jesus answered them, Verily, verily, I say unto you, Whosoever *continueth to* committeth sin is the servant of sin.
35.   And the servant *of any master* abideth not in the house forever *because he is not a part of the family*. But the Son *of the master* abideth *within the house for*ever.
36.   If the Son *of God* therefore shall make you free *through his redemption provision*, ye shall be free indeed.
37.   I know that ye are *of* Abraham's seed *according to the flesh;* but ye *that believeth not on me* seek to kill me, because my word hath no place in you.
38.   I speak *only* that which I have seen with my *Heavenly* Father. And ye do that which ye have seen with your father, *the Devil*.
39.   They answered and said unto him, Abraham is our father. Jesus saith unto them, If ye *really* were Abraham's children *spiritually*, ye would do the works of Abraham.
40.   But now ye seek to kill me, a man that hath told you the truth, which I have heard of God. This did not Abraham.

JOHN 8:50

41. *Ye continue to* **do the deeds of your father. Then said they to him, We be not born of fornication; we have** *only* **one Father, even God.**

42. **Jesus said unto them, If God were** *really* **your Father, ye would love me. For I proceeded forth and came from God; neither came I of myself, but he sent me.**

43. **Why do ye not understand my speech? Even because ye cannot hear my word.**

44. **Ye are of your** *spiritual* **father the Devil, and the lusts of your** *spiritual* **father ye will do. He was a murderer from the beginning, and** *he* **abode not in the truth, because there is no truth in him. When he speaketh** *it is* **a lie,** *and* **he speaketh of his own; for he is a** *continual* **liar, and the father of it.**

45. **And because I** *purpose to* **tell you the truth, ye believe me not.**

46. **Which of you** *is able to* **convinceth me of sin? And if I say the truth, why do ye not believe me?**

47. **He that is** *spiritually* **of God heareth God's words. Ye therefore hear them not, because ye are not** *spiritually* **of God.**

48. Then answered the Jews, and said unto him, Say we not well that thou art *in truth* **a Samaritan, and hast a devil?**

49. **Jesus answered, I have not a devil. But I honour my** *Heavenly* **Father, and ye do dishonor me.**

50. **And I seek not mine own** *personal* **glory. There is one that seeketh and judgeth.**

51. **Verily, verily, I say unto you, If a man keep my saying, he shall never see** *Eternal Spiritual* **Death.**

52.   Then said the Jews unto him, Now we know *and are sure* that thou hast a devil. Abraham *our father* is dead, and the prophets *that came after him are dead.* And thou sayest, If a man keep my saying, he shall never taste of *Physical* Death.

53.   Art thou greater than our father Abraham, which is *Physically* Dead? And *greater than* the prophets *which* are *Physically* Dead? Whom makest thou thyself *to be?*

54.   Jesus answered, If I honour myself, *then* my honour is nothing. It is my Heavenly Father that honoureth me, of whom ye say, that he is your God.

55.   Yet ye have not *ever* known him. But I know him, and if I should say *that* I know him not, I shall be a liar *just* like unto you. But I *do* know him, and keep his saying.

56.   Your father Abraham rejoiced to see my day: and he saw it *in a vision*, and was glad.

57.   Then said the Jews unto him, Thou art not yet fifty years old, and hast thou seen Abraham *our father?*

58.   Jesus said unto them, Verily, verily, I say unto you, Before *your father* Abraham was, I Am.

59.   Then took they up stones to cast at him. But Jesus hid himself, and *then* went out of the temple, *even* going through the midst of them. And so *he* passed by *them.*

CHAPTER 9

1. And as Jesus *later on* passed by, he saw a man which was blind from his birth.
2. And his disciples asked him, saying, Master, who did sin, this man or his parents, that he was born blind?
3. Jesus answered, Neither hath this man sinned, nor his parents. But that the works of God should be made manifest in him.
4. I must work the works of him that sent me, while it is *still* day. The night *soon* cometh, when no man can work.
5. As long as I am in the world, I am the *Given* Light of the world.
6. When he had thus spoken, he spat on the ground, and made clay of the spittle, and *then* he anointed the eyes of the blind man with the clay.
7. And said unto him, *utilizing the Holy Spirit given Gifts of Healing,* Go, wash in the pool of Siloam, (which is *meaning* by interpretation, Sent). So he went his way therefore, and washed *his eyes in the pool,* and *then* came *back* seeing.
8. The neighbors therefore, and they which before had seen him *and knew* that he *really* was blind, said, is not this he that sat and begged *for a living?*
9. Some said, *Yes,* this is he. Others said, He is like *unto* him. But he *himself* said, I am he.
10. Therefore said they unto him, How were thine eyes opened?

11.   *He answered and said, A man that is called Jesus made* some *clay, and* came and *anointed mine eyes, and said unto me,* Go to the pool of Siloam, and wash. *And I went* to the pool *and washed, and I received* my *sight.*

12.   *Then said they unto him, Where is he* now? *He said, I know not* where he is.

13.   Then *they brought to the Pharisees him that aforetime was blind.*

14.   *And it was the Sabbath Day* of Commandment *when Jesus* had *made the clay, and opened his eyes.*

15.   *Then again, the Pharisees also asked him how he had received his sight. He said unto them, He put clay upon mine eyes, and I* went and *washed, and do* now *see.*

16.   *Therefore said some of the* unbelieving *Pharisees, this man is not of God, because he keepeth not the Sabbath Day* of Commandment, according to the Law of Moses. *Others said, How* then *can a man that is a sinner do such miracles? And there was a division* that developed *among them.*

17.   *They say unto the blind man* once *again, What sayest thou of him, that he hath opened thine eyes? He said, His is a prophet* of God.

18.   *But the* judgmental *Jews did not believe concerning him, that he had* once *been blind, and received his sight, until they called the parents of him that had received his sight.*

19.   *And they asked* of *them, saying Is this your son, who ye say was born blind? How then doth he now see?*

20. *His parents answered them and said,* **We know that this** *really* **is our son, and that he** *really* **was born blind.**

21. *But by what means he* **is** *now able to* **seeth, we know not. Or who** *it is that* **hath opened his eyes, we know not. He is of** *full* **age; ask him** *directly,* **he shall speak for himself.**

22. **These words spake his parents, because they feared the** *unbelieving* **Jews. For the** *unbelieving* **Jews had agreed already** *among themselves,* **that if any man did confess that he was** *the* **Christ, he should be put out of the synagogue.**

23. **Therefore said his parents, He is of** *full* **age; ask him.**

24. **Then again called they** *back* **the man that was blind, and said unto him, Give God the praise** *for what has been done.* **We know that this man is a sinner.**

25. *He answered and said* **unto** *them,* **Whether he be a sinner or no, I know not. One thing I** *do* **know, that, whereas I was** *once* **blind,** *but* **now I see.**

26. **Then said they to him again,** *Tell us once more,* **what did he to thee? How opened he thine eyes?**

27. *He answered them,* **I have told you already, and ye did not hear** *what I said?* **Wherefore would ye** *want to* **hear it again? Will ye also become his disciples?**

28. **Then they reviled him, and said, Thou art his disciple** *maybe;* **but we are Moses' disciples.**

29. **We know that God spake unto Moses.** *But* **as for this fellow, we know not from whence he is.**

30. The man *surprisingly* answered and said unto them, Why herein is a marvelous thing *indeed*, that ye know not from whence he is, and yet he hath opened mine eyes.
31. Now we *all* know that God heareth not sinners *when they pray*. But if any man be a worshipper of God, and doeth his will, him he heareth.
32. Since the world began was it not heard that any *common* man opened the eyes of one that was born blind.
33. If this man were not of God, he could *really* do nothing.
34. They answered and said unto him, Thou wast altogether born in sins, and dost thou *presume to* teach us? And they cast him out.
35. Jesus heard that they had cast him out. And when he had found him, he said unto him, Dost thou believe on the Son of God?
36. He answered and said, Who is he, Lord, that I might believe on him?
37. And Jesus said unto him, Thou hast both seen him *with thine eyes*, and it is he that talketh with thee.
38. And he said, Lord, I *do* believe. And he worshipped him.
39. And Jesus said, For judgment *of evil* I am come into this world, that they which see not might *truly* see; and that they which *think that they* see might be made blind.
40. And some of the Pharisees which were with him heard these words, and said unto him, Are we blind also?

JOHN 10:8

41. **Jesus said unto them,** *If ye were* really spiritually *blind, ye should have no sin. But now ye say, We* spiritually *see; therefore your sin remaineth.*

CHAPTER 10

1. *Verily, verily, I say unto you, He that* attempts to *entereth not by the door into the sheepfold, but* rather *climbeth up some other way, the same is a thief and a robber.*
2. *But he that* genuinely *entereth in by the door, is the* rightful *shepherd of the sheep.*
3. *To him the* appointed *porter openeth* widely*; and the sheep hear his voice. And he calleth his own sheep by name, and leadeth them out.*
4. *And when he putteth forth his own sheep, he* then *goeth before them, and the sheep follow him: for they know his voice.*
5. *And a stranger will they not follow, but will flee from him. For they know not the voice of strangers.*
6. **This parable spake Jesus unto them; but they understood not what things they were which he spake unto them** about**.**
7. **Then said Jesus unto them again,** *Verily, verily, I say unto you, I am The Door of the* Jewish *sheep.*
8. *All that ever came before me are thieves and robbers* and false Messiahs*. But the sheep did not hear them.*

JOHN 10:9

9. *I am The Door. By me if any man enter*eth *there*in, *he shall be saved* from Everlasting Destruction, *and shall go in and out, and find pasture.*

10. *The thief cometh not, but for to steal, and to kill, and to destroy. I am come that they might have* Everlasting **Life***, and that they might have it more abundantly* even now*.*

11. *I am the Good Shepherd. The Good Shepherd* shall *giveth his life for the* Jewish *sheep.*

12. *But he that is* only *a hireling, and not the shepherd, whose own the sheep are not, seeth the wolf coming, and leaveth the sheep* alone*, and fleeth. And the wolf catcheth them, and scattereth the sheep.*

13. *The hireling fleeth, because he is* only *a hireling, and careth not for the sheep.*

14. *I am the Good Shepherd, and I know my sheep, and am known of mine.*

15. *As the* Heavenly **Father** *knoweth me, even so know I the* Heavenly **Father***. And I* am come to **lay down my life for the** Jewish **sheep***.*

16. *And other* Gentile *sheep I have, which are not of this fold. Them also I must bring and they shall hear my voice. And there shall be* only *one fold, and one shepherd.*

17. *Therefore doth my* Heavenly **Father** *love me, because I lay down my life, that I might take it again* at my resurrection*.*

18. *No man taketh it from me, but I lay it down of myself. I have* the *power to lay it down, and I have* the *power to take it* once *again. This commandment have I received of my* Heavenly **Father***.*

19. **There was a division therefore** once **again among the Jews for these sayings.**
20. **And many of them said, He hath a devil, and** he **is mad. Why hear ye him?**
21. **Others said, These are not the words of him that hath a devil. Can a** man which hath a **devil open the eyes of the blind?**
22. **And it was at Jerusalem** and **the Feast of the Dedication** that these things happened. **And it was** the **winter** season.
23. **And Jesus walked** with**in the temple** with**in Solomon's porch.**
24. **Then came the Jews round about him** again, **and said unto him, How long dost thou make us to doubt? If thou be the Christ** that is to come, **tell us** then **plainly.**
25. **Jesus answered them,** I have already **told you, and ye believed** me **not. The** very **works that I do in my** Heavenly **Father's name, they** also **bear witness of me.**
26. **But ye believe** me **not, because ye are not of my sheep, as I** have **said unto you.**
27. **My sheep hear my voice, and I know them, and they follow me.**
28. **And I** shall **give unto them Eternal Life, and they shall never perish, neither shall any man pluck them out of my hand.**
29. **My** Heavenly **Father, which gave them** to **me, is greater than all. And no man is able to pluck them out of my** Heavenly **Father's hand.**
30. **I and my** Heavenly **Father are one.**

31. **Then the Jews took up stones again to stone him.**

32. **Jesus answered them,** Many good works have I shown *unto* you from my *Heavenly* Father. For which of those works do ye *now* stone me?

33. **The Jews answered him, saying, For a good work we stone thee not, but for blasphemy. And because that thou, being** *only* **a man, makest thyself** *to be* **God.**

34. Jesus answered them, Is it not written in your law, "I said, Ye are gods?" *(Psalm 82:6)*

35. If he called them gods, unto whom the word of God came, *that is the Jewish people;* and the Scripture cannot be broken;

36. Say ye of him, whom the *Heavenly* Father hath sanctified, and sent into the world, Thou blasphemeth; because I said, I am the Son of God?

37. If I do not the works of my *Heavenly* Father, *then* believe me not.

38. But if I do *what he hath sent me to do*, though ye believe not me, believe the works *that ye see*. That ye may know and believe, that the *Heavenly* Father is *dwelling* in me, and I *am dwelling* in him.

39. **Therefore they sought again to take him** *by force;* **but he escaped out of their hand.**

40. **And** *he* **went away again beyond** *the* **Jordan River into the place** *called Bethabara,* **where John at first baptized** *people.* **And there he abode.**

41. **And many** *people* **resorted unto him and said, John did no miracle, but all things that John spake of this man** *when he bore witness of him,* **were true.**

42. **And many** *did* **believed on him there.**

CHAPTER 11

1.   Now a certain man was sick, *who was* named Lazarus, of Bethany, the town of Mary and her sister Martha.

2.   (It was that Mary which *had* anointed the Lord with ointment *in the house of Simon the Leper*, and wiped his feet with her hair, whose brother Lazarus was sick.)

3.   Therefore his sisters sent unto him; saying, Lord, behold, he whom thou lovest is sick.

4.   When Jesus heard that, *under the operation of the Holy Spirit gifting of the Word of Knowledge*, he said, This sickness is not unto death, but for the glory of God *to be manifest*, that the Son of God might be glorified thereby.

5.   Now Jesus dearly loved Martha, and her sister *Mary*, and Lazarus *their brother*.

6.   When he had heard therefore that he was sick, he abode two days still in the same place where he was.

7.   Then after that, *under the unction of the Holy Spirit*, saith he *un*to his disciples, Let us go into Judea again.

8.   *His disciples say unto him, Master, the Jews of late sought to stone thee* there; *and goest thou thither again?*

9.   *Jesus answered,* Are there not twelve hours in the day? If any man walk in the day*time,* he shall *stumbleth not, because he* clearly *seeth the light of this world.*

10.   But if a man walk in the night*time,* he shall *stumbleth, because there is no light* dwelling with*in him.*

11.   *These things said he* unto them. *And after that, he saith unto them,* Our friend Lazarus sleepeth just like Jairus' daughter did; *but I go, that I may awake him out of* that *sleep.*

12.   *Then said his disciples,* thinking only of the natural, *Lord, if he sleep, he shall do well.*

13.   *Howbeit Jesus spake* to them *of his death. But they thought that he had spoken of taking of rest* as *in sleep.*

14.   *Then said Jesus unto them plainly,* Lazarus is dead.

15.   And I am glad for your sakes that I was not there, to the intent that ye may finally believe. Nevertheless, let us go unto him.

16.   *Then said Thomas, which is called Didymus,* rather rashly *unto his fellow disciples,* not really considering what he was saying, *Let us also go, that we may die with him.*

17.   *Then when Jesus came* near to Lazarus' house, *he found that he had lain in the grave* for *four days already.*

JOHN 11:27

18. **Now Bethany was nigh unto Jerusalem,** *only about fifteen furlongs off.*

19. **And many of the Jews came to Martha and Mary** *because they knew the family*, **to comfort them concerning their brother.**

20. **Then Martha, as soon as she heard that Jesus was coming, went** *out of the house*, **and met him. But Mary sat** *silent with***in the house.**

21. **Then said Martha unto Jesus, Lord, if thou hadst been here,** *thou wouldst have laid your hands upon him, and* **my brother had not died.**

22. **But I know** *and have confidence*, **that even now, whatsoever thou wilt ask of God, God will give it** *unto* **thee.**

23. **Jesus saith unto her,** *Take heart,* **thy brother shall rise again.**

24. **Martha saith unto him,** *Lord,* **I know that he shall rise again in the resurrection** *unto life*, **at the last day.**

25. **Jesus said unto her,** *Martha, please understand,* **I am The Resurrection, and The Life. He that believeth in me,** *even* **though he were dead, yet shall he live.**

26. **And whosoever liveth and believeth in me shall never die. Believeth thou this?**

27. **She**, *still not understanding*, **saith unto him, Yea Lord. I believe that thou art the Christ, the Son of God, which should come into the world** *and rescue us from the Roman occupation.*

28. And when she had so said, she went her way *back into the house*, and called Mary her sister *and whispered* secretly, saying, The Master is come, and calleth for thee.

29. As soon as she *had* heard that, she arose quickly, and came unto him.

30. Now Jesus was not yet come into the town, but was *still* in that place where Martha *had* met him.

31. The *local* Jews then which were with her in the house, and comforted her, when they saw Mary, that she rose up hastily and went *right* out, followed her, saying, She goeth unto the grave *for* to weep there.

32. Then when Mary was come *to* where Jesus was, and saw him, she fell down *straightway* at his feet, saying unto him, Lord , if thou hadst been here, *thou wouldst have laid your hands upon him, and* my brother had not died.

33. When Jesus therefore saw her weeping, and the *local* Jews also weeping which came with her, he *was moved and* groaned *with*in the spirit, and was *indeed* troubled.

34. And *he* said *unto them*, Where have ye laid him? They say unto him, Lord, *he is in the sepulcher,* come and see.

35. Jesus *then* wept.

36. Then said the *local* Jews, Behold how he loved him!

JOHN 11:44

37. And some of them said, Could not this man, which *has* opened the eyes of the blind, have caused that even this *good* man *Lazarus* should not have died?

38. Jesus therefore again groaning *with*in himself cometh to the grave. It was a cave, and a stone lay upon it.

39. Jesus said, Take ye away the stone. Martha, the sister of him that was dead, saith unto him, Lord, by this time *his spirit hath departed and* he stinketh; for he hath been dead *for* four days *now*.

40. Jesus saith unto her, Said I not unto thee, that, if thou wouldest believe, thou shouldest see the glory of God?

41. Then they took away the stone from the place where the dead was laid. And Jesus lifted up his eyes *towards Heaven*, and said, *Heavenly* Father, I thank thee that thou hast heard me.

42. And I knew that thou hearest me always. But because of the people which stand by *have* I said it, that they may believe that thou hast sent me.

43. And when he thus had spoken, *under the Holy Spirit gifting of the Working of Miracles,* he cried with a loud voice, Lazarus, come forth.

44. And he that was dead came forth, bound *both* hand and foot with graveclothes. And his face was bound about with a napkin. Jesus *then* saith unto them *that were closest to him*, Loose him, and let him go.

JOHN 11:45

45. Then many of the *local* Jews which came to Mary, and had seen the things which Jesus did, believed on him.

46. But some of them *which did not like Jesus*, went their ways to the Pharisees, and told *unto* them what things *that* Jesus had done.

47. Then gathered *together* the chief priests and the Pharisees a council, and said, What do we *now?* For this man *Jesus* doeth many miracles.

48. If we *shall* let him thus alone, all men will *soon* believe on him. And the Romans shall come and take away both our *personal* place *of prestige* and *our* national *standing.*

49. And one of them, named Caiaphas, being the High Priest that same year, said unto them, Ye know nothing at all.

50. Nor *even* consider that it is expedient for us, that one man should die for the people, and that the whole nation perish not.

51. And this spake he not of himself; but being High Priest that *same* year, he prophesied *under the operation of the Holy Spirit gifting of Prophecy* that Jesus should die for that *particular* nation.

52. And not for that *particular* nation only, but that also, *after his resurrection,* he should gather together into one *body* the children of God that were scattered abroad *at that time.*

53. Then, from that day forth, they took counsel together for to put him to death.

54. *Jesus therefore walked no more openly among the Jews.* But went thence unto a country *that was* **near to the wilderness, into a city called Ephraim, and there** he **continued with his disciples.**
55. **And the Jews' Passover** Celebration **was nigh at hand.** And **many went out of the** surrounding **countryside up to Jerusalem before the Passover** Celebration, in order **to purify themselves.**
56. **Then sought they** diligently **for Jesus, and spake among themselves, as they stood** there **in the temple, What think ye, that he will not come to the feast?**
57. **Now both the chief priests and the Pharisees had given a commandment** to the temple guards and others, **that, if any man knew where he were, he should show it, that they might take him.**

CHAPTER 12

1. **Then Jesus, six days before the Passover** Celebration, **came to Bethany where Lazarus was** living; **which had been dead,** but **whom he** had **raised from the dead.**
2. **There they made him a supper; and Martha** was the one that **served** the supper. **But Lazarus was one of them that sat at the table with him.**
3. **Then took** Lazarus' sister **Mary, a pound of Ointment of Spikenard,** which was **very costly, and once again anointed the feet of Jesus and wiped his feet with her hair. And the house was filled with the** sweet **ordour of the ointment.**

4. **Then saith one of his disciples,** *namely* **Judas Iscariot, Simon's son, which** *later on* **should betray him,**

5. **Why was not this ointment sold for three hundred pence, and** *the money then* **given to the poor?**

6. **This he said, not that he** *really* **cared for the poor; but because he was a thief, and** *he* **had the** *responsibility of holding the* **bag** *of resources***, and** *he* **bare what was put therein.**

7. **Then said Jesus,** *Let her alone: for against the day of my burying hath she kept this.*

8. *For the poor always ye have with you; but me ye have not always.*

9. **Much people of the** *local* **Jews therefore knew that he was there** *at the house.* **And they came** *to the house* **not for Jesus' sake only, but that they might see Lazarus also, whom he had raised from the dead.**

10. **But the chief priests consulted** *together* **that they might put Lazarus also to death;**

11. **Because that by reason of him** *being raised from the dead* **many of the** *local* **Jews went away, and believed on Jesus.**

12. **On the next day much people that were come to the** *Passover* **Feast, when they** *had* **heard that Jesus was** *going to be* **coming to Jerusalem,**

13. **Took branches of** *the* **palm trees, and went forth to meet him, and cried** *aloud,* **Hosanna: Blessed is the King of Israel that cometh in the name of the Lord.**

14.   And Jesus, when he had found a young ass, sat thereon; as it is written *in the Book of Zechariah*,

15.   "Fear not, O daughter of Zion. Behold, thy King cometh, sitting on an ass's colt." *(Zechariah 9:9)*

16.   These things understood not his disciples at the first. But *after his resurrection,* when Jesus was glorified, then remembered they that these things were written of him, and that they had done these things unto him.

17.   The people therefore that was with him when he called Lazarus out of his grave, and raised him *up* from the dead, bare record.

18.   For this cause the people also met him, for that they *had* heard that he had done this miracle.

19.   The Pharisees therefore said among themselves, Perceive ye how ye prevail nothing? Behold, the *whole* world is gone after him.

20.   And there were certain *Jewish* Greeks among them that came up to worship at the feast.

21.   The same came therefore to Philip, which was of Bethsaida of Galilee, and desired him, saying, Sir, we would *like to* see Jesus.

22.   Philip cometh and telleth Andrew. And again Andrew and Philip *cometh and* tell Jesus.

23.   And Jesus answered them, saying, The hour is come, that the Son of man should be glorified.

24.   Verily, verily, I say unto you, Except a corn of wheat *should* fall into the ground and die, it abideth alone. But if it die, it bringeth forth much fruit.

25. *He that loveth his* natural *life shall lose it. And he that hateth his* natural *life in this world shall keep it unto Life Eternal.*

26. *If any man* will *serve me,* then *let him follow me. And where I am, there shall also my servant be. If any man* will *serve me, him will my* Heavenly *Father honour.*

27. *Now is my soul troubled; and what shall I say?* Heavenly *Father, save me from this hour! But* it is *for this cause came I unto this hour.*

28. Heavenly *Father, glorify thy name.* **Then came there a voice from heaven, saying, "I have both glorified it, and will glorify it** once **again."**

29. **The people therefore that stood by, and heard it, said that it thundered. Others said** that **an angel spake** unto **him.**

30. **Jesus answered and said,** *This voice came not because of me, but for your sakes.*

31. *Now is the judgment of this world* come. *Now shall the prince* of the power of the air, *of this world be cast out.*

32. *And I, if I be lifted up from the earth* by crucifixion, *I will draw all men unto me.*

33. **This he said, signifying** by **what death he should die.**

34. **The** gathered **people answered him, We have heard out of the Law** of Moses **that Christ abideth forever. And how sayest thou,** that **the Son of man must be lifted up? Who is this Son of man?**

35. *Then Jesus said unto them,* Yet a little while is the Given Light with you. Walk clearly while ye have the Given Light, lest the darkness suddenly cometh upon you. For he that walketh in the darkness knoweth not whither he goeth.

36. While ye have the Given Light, believe in the Light, that ye may become the children of Light. *These things spake Jesus, and departed, and did hide himself from them.*

37. *But though he had done so many miracles before them, yet they believed not on him.*

38. *That the saying of Isaiah the prophet might be fulfilled, which he spake, "Lord, who hath believed our report? And to whom hath the arm of the Lord been revealed?"* (Isaiah 53:1)

39. *Therefore they could not believe, because that Isaiah said again,*

40. *"He, that is, the Devil,* **hath blinded their** *spiritual* **eyes, and** *hath* **hardened their heart; that they should not** *be able to* **see with their** *spiritual* **eyes, nor understand with their heart, and be**come **converted, and I should heal them."** (Isaiah 6:10)

41. *These things said Isaiah, when he saw his glory in a vision, and spake of him.*

42. *Nevertheless among the chief rulers also many believed on him; but because of the controlling influence of the* **Pharisees** *they did not confess him* openly, *lest they should be put out of the synagogue.*

43. *For they* sadly *loved the praises of men more than the praise of God.*

44. ***Jesus cried*** *aloud* ***and said,*** **He that believeth on me,** *actually* **believeth not on me, but on him that sent me.**

45. **And he that seeth me seeth him that sent me.**

46. **I am come** *as a Given* **Light into the world, that whosoever believeth on me should not** *continue to* **abide in darkness.**

47. **And if any man hear my words, and believe not, I** *personally* **judge him not. For,** *at this time,* **I came** *into the world,* **not to judge the world, but to save the world.**

48. **He that** *personally* **rejecteth me, and receiveth not my words, hath one that judgeth him. The word that I have spoken,** *which is the written Word of God,* **the same shall judge him in the last day.**

49. **For I have not** *personally* **spoken of myself, but the** *Heavenly* **Father which sent me, he gave me a commandment,** *of* **what I should say, and** *of* **what I should speak.**

50. **And I know** *within my spirit* **that his commandment is** *unto* **Life Everlasting. Whatsoever I speak therefore, even as the** *Heavenly* **Father** *has* **said unto me, so** *then will* **I speak.**

CHAPTER 13

1. **Now** *just* **before the feast of the Passover** *Celebration,* **when Jesus knew**, *by the Holy Spirit gifting of the Word of Knowledge,* **that his hour was** *now* **come that he should depart out of this world**, *and return* **unto the** *Heavenly* **Father; having loved his own** *brethren* **which were in the world, he loved them** *right up* **unto the end.**

2. **And** *the Last* **Supper being ended, the Devil having now put into the heart of Judas Iscariot, Simon's son to betray him;**

3. **Jesus knowing** *within his spirit* **that the** *Heavenly* **Father had given all things into his hands, and that he was** *originally* **come from God, and** *now* **went** *back* **to God;**

4. **He riseth from** *the* **supper, and laid aside his garments; and took a towel, and girded himself.**

5. **After that, he poureth water into a basin, and began to wash** *each of* **the disciples' feet,** *including those of Judas Iscariot,* **and to wipe them** *dry* **with the towel wherewith he was girded.**

6. **Then cometh he to Simon Peter. And Peter saith unto him, Lord, dost thou wash my feet?**

7. **Jesus answered and said unto him,** What I do thou knowest not now; but thou shalt know hereafter.

8. **Peter saith unto him, Thou shalt never wash my feet** *Lord.* **Jesus answered him,** If I wash thee not, *then* thou hast no part with me.

JOHN 13:9

9. **Simon Peter** *quickly repented and* **saith unto him, Lord, not my feet only, but also my hands and my head.**

10. **Jesus saith** *unto* **him,** He that is washed *by me* needeth not, save to wash his feet, but *in doing so* is clean every whit. And ye are *now* clean, but not all.

11. **For he knew who should** *shortly* **betray him; therefore said he,** Ye are not all clean.

12. **So after** *that* **he had washed their feet, and had taken** *back* **his garments, and was set down again, he said unto them,** Know ye what I have done *unto you?*

13. **Ye call me Master and Lord: and ye say well; for so I am.**

14. If I then, your Lord and Master, have washed your feet; ye also ought to wash one another's feet.

15. For I have given *unto* you an example, that ye should do *to one another* as I have done *unto you.*

16. **Verily, verily, I say unto you,** The servant *within any house* **is not greater than his lord;** *and* **neither** *is* **he that is sent greater than he that sent him.**

17. If ye know these things, happy are ye *to be,* if ye do them.

18. I speak not of you all. For I know whom I have chosen. But that the Scripture *in the Book of Psalms* may be fulfilled, "He that eateth bread with me hath lifted up his heel against me." *(Psalms 41:9)*

19. Now I tell you before it *is* come, that, when it is come to pass, ye may believe that I Am.

20. **Verily, verily, I say unto you, He that receiveth whomsoever I** *shall* **send receiveth me; and he that receiveth me** *shall* **receiveth him that sent me.**

JOHN 12:29

21.   When Jesus had thus said, he was troubled *with*in *his* **spirit, and testified, and said,** Verily, verily, I say unto you, that one of you shall betray me.

22.   **Then the disciples looked one on another, doubting of whom** *it might be that* **he spake.**

23.   **Now there was leaning on Jesus' bosom one of his disciples, whom Jesus loved** *named John*.

24.   **Simon Peter therefore beckoned** *unto* **him, that he should ask** *Jesus* **who it should be of whom he spake.**

25.   **He then lying on Jesus' breast saith unto him, Lord, who is it?**

26.   **Jesus answered,** He it is, to whom I shall give a sop, when I have dipped it *into the dish*. **And when he had dipped the sop, he gave it to Judas Iscariot, the son of Simon.**

27.   **And after the sop** *was given* **Satan entered into him** *by interpenetration to unify the league of Judas' intent of betrayal. (As a Celestial Bodied angel, Satan cannot actually enter into and possess any Human Being)* **Then said Jesus unto him,** That thou doest, do quickly.

28.   **Now no man at the table** *really* **knew for what intent he spake this unto him.**

29.   **For some of them thought, because** *that* **Judas had the bag** *containing the money*, **that Jesus had said unto him,** Buy those things that we have need of against the feast; **or, that he should give something to the poor.**

30. He then, having received the sop *and his instructions*, went immediately out. And it was *now the* night*time*.

31. Therefore, when he was gone out, Jesus said, Now is the Son of man *to be* glorified, and God is glorified in him.

32. *And* **if God be glorified in him,** *then* **God shall also glorify him in himself, and shall straightway glorify him.**

33. **Little children, yet** *only* **a little while** *longer* **I am with you. Ye shall seek** *for* **me, and as I said unto the Jews, Whither I go, ye cannot come. So now I say** *un*t**o you.**

34. **A New Commandment I give unto you, That ye love one another. As I have loved you, that ye also** *should* **love one another.**

35. **By this shall all men know that ye are my disciples, if ye have love one to another.**

36. Simon Peter said unto him, Lord, whither goest thou? Jesus answered him, **Whither I go, thou canst not follow me now; but thou shalt follow me afterward.**

37. Peter said unto him, Lord, why cannot I follow thee now? I will lay down my life for thy sake.

38. Jesus, *by virtue of the Holy Spirit gifting of the Word of Knowledge,* answered him, **Wilt thou** *really* **lay down thy life for my sake? Verily, verily, I say unto thee, The cock shall not crow, till thou hast denied me thrice.**

CHAPTER 14

1. *Jesus, continuing to minister, saith,* **Let not your heart be troubled. Ye believe in God, believe also in me.**

2. **In my Father's house are many mansions. If it were not so, I would have told you. I** *now* **go to prepare a place for you.**

3. **And if I go and prepare a place for you, I will** *then* **come again, and receive you unto myself;** *so* **that where I am, there ye may be also.**

4. **And whither I go ye know** *down in your heart,* **and the way ye know.**

5. *Doubting* **Thomas saith unto him, Lord, we know not whither thou** *now* **goest; and how can we know the way?**

6. **Jesus saith unto him,** **I am the Way, the Truth, and the Life.** *And* **no man cometh unto the** *Heavenly* **Father, but by me.**

7. **If ye had** *really* **known me,** *then* **ye should have known my** *Heavenly* **Father also. And from henceforth ye** *shall* **know him, and** *ye* **have seen him.**

8. **Philip saith unto him, Lord,** *just* **show** *unto* **us the** *Heavenly* **Father, and it sufficeth us.**

9. **Jesus saith unto him,** **Have I been so long** *a* **time with you, and yet hast thou** *really* **not known me, Philip? He that hath seen me hath** *already* **seen the** *Heavenly* **Father. And how sayest thou then, Show** *unto* **us the** *Heavenly* **Father?**

10. Believest thou not that I am in the Heavenly Father, and that the Father is in me? The very words that I speak unto you I speak not of myself, but the Heavenly Father that dwelleth in me by his Spirit, he doeth the works.

11. Believe me that I am in the Heavenly Father and the Heavenly Father is in me: or else believe me for the very works' sake.

12. Verily, verily, I say unto you, He that believeth on me, the works that I now do, shall he do also. And greater works than these shall he do, because I now go unto my Heavenly Father.

13. And whatsoever ye shall ask in my name, that will I do for you, that the Heavenly Father may be glorified in the Son.

14. If ye shall ask any thing in my name, I will do it for you.

15. If ye love me, then keep my commandments.

16. And I will pray the Heavenly Father, and he shall give unto you another Comforter other than me, that he may abide with you forever.

17. Even the Spirit of Truth himself; whom the world cannot receive, because it seeth him not with their eyes, neither knoweth him in their heart. But ye shall know him, for he dwelleth with you right now, and shall be dwelling within you because of your New Birth.

18. I will not leave you comfortless. I will come unto you.

19. Yet a little while, and the world seeth me no more after the flesh. But ye shall see me. And because I shall live, ye shall live also.

20. At that day ye shall know that I am in my Heavenly Father, and ye are in me, and I am in you.

21. He that hath my Royal Law Commandments, and keepeth them, he it is that loveth me. And he that loveth me shall be loved of my Heavenly Father, and I will love him, and will manifest myself to him.

22. Judas the brother of James saith unto him, not Iscariot, Lord, how is it that thou wilt manifest thyself unto us, and not unto the world?

23. Jesus answered and said unto him, If a man love me, he will keep my words. And my Heavenly Father will love him, and we will come unto him, and will make our abode with him.

24. He that loveth me not, keepeth not my sayings. And the word which ye hear from me is not mine, but the Heavenly Father's which sent me.

25. These things have I spoken unto you, being yet present with you.

26. But the Comforter, which is the Holy Ghost, whom the Heavenly Father will send unto you in my name, he shall teach you all things that ye need to know, and shall bring all things to your remembrance, of whatsoever I have said unto you.

27. My peace I leave with you, my peace I give unto you. Not as the world giveth, give I unto you. Let not your heart be troubled, neither let it be afraid.

28. Ye have heard how I said unto you, *that* I go away, and *will* come again unto you. If ye loved me, ye would rejoice because I said, I go unto the *Heavenly* Father. For my *Heavenly* Father, *as God*, is greater than I *am, as a Man*.

29. And now I have told you before it comes to pass, that, when it is come to pass, ye might believe.

30. Hereafter I will not talk *very* much with you. For the prince of this world cometh, and hath nothing in me *that he can lay hold of*.

31. But that the world may know that I love the *Heavenly* Father. And as the *Heavenly* Father gave me *a* commandment, even so I do. Arise, let us go hence.

CHAPTER 15

1. *Jesus also ministered unto his disciples, saying,* I am the True Vine, and my Father is the husbandman.

2. Every branch *proclaiming to be* in me that beareth not fruit, he taketh away. And every branch *proclaiming to be in me* that beareth fruit, he purgeth it, that it may bring forth more fruit.

3. Now ye are clean through the word which I have spoken unto you.

4. *Continue to* abide in me, and I *will continue to abide* in you. As the branch *on the vine* cannot bear fruit of itself, except it abide in the vine, no more can ye *beareth fruit*, except ye abide in me.

5.   *I am the vine, ye are the branches. He that* continueth to *abideth in me, and I in him, the same bringeth forth much fruit, for without me ye can do nothing.*
6.   *If a man* continually *abideth not in me, he is cast forth as a* severed *branch, and is* become *withered. And men* shall *gather them, and* shall *cast them into the fire, and they are* to be *burned.*
7.   *If ye* shall continue to *abide in me, and my words abide in you, ye shall ask what ye will, and it shall be done unto you.*
8.   *Herein is my* Heavenly *Father glorified, that ye bear much fruit. So shall ye be my disciples.*
9.   *As the* Heavenly *Father hath loved me, so have I loved you. Continue ye in my love.*
10.   *If ye keep my* Royal Law *Commandments, ye shall* indeed *abide in my love. Even as I have kept my* Heavenly *Father's commandments, and* so *abide in his love.*
11.   *These things have I spoken unto you, that my joy might remain in you, and that your joy might be full.*
12.   *This is my* Royal Law *Commandment, That ye love one another, as I have loved you.*
13.   *Greater love hath no man than this that a man lay down his life for his friends.*
14.   *Ye are my friends, if ye do whatsoever I command you.*

15. Henceforth I call you not servants; for the servant knoweth not what his lord doeth. But I have called you friends; for all things that I have heard of my Heavenly Father I have made known unto you.

16. Ye have not chosen me, but I have chosen you, and ordained you, that ye should go and bring forth spiritual fruit, and that your spiritual fruit should remain. That whatsoever ye shall ask of the Heavenly Father in my name, he may give it unto you.

17. These things I command you, that ye love one another.

18. If the world hates you marvel not, ye know that it hated me before it hated you.

19. If ye were still of the world, the world would love his own. But because ye are not of the world anymore, but I have chosen you out of the world, therefore the world hateth you.

20. Remember the word that I said unto you, The servant is not greater than his lord. If they have persecuted me, they will also persecute you. If they have kept my saying, they will keep yours also.

21. But all these things will they do unto you for my name's sake, because they know not him that sent me.

22. If I had not come into this world and spoken unto them, they had not had any sin. But now they have no cloak for their sin anymore.

23. He that hateth me hateth my Heavenly Father also.

24. *If I had not done among them the works which none other man did, they had not had* any *sin. But now have they both seen and hated both me and my* Heavenly *Father.*

25. *But this cometh to pass, that the word might be fulfilled that is written in their law, "They hated me without a cause."* *(Psalms 35:19; 69:4)*

26. *But when the Comforter is come whom I will send unto you from the* Heavenly *Father, even the Spirit of Truth, which proceedeth* forth *from the* Heavenly *Father, he shall testify of me.*

27. *And ye also shall bear* me *witness, because ye have been with me from the beginning.*

CHAPTER 16

1. *These things have I spoken unto you, that ye should not be offended* when the time comes.

2. *They shall put you out of the synagogues. Yea, the time cometh, that whosoever* shall *killeth you will think that he doeth God service.*

3. *And these things will they do unto you, because they have not known the* Heavenly *Father, nor me* his Only Begotten Son.

4. *But these things have I told you* now, *that when the time shall come, ye may remember that I told you of them. And these things I said not unto you at the beginning* of our walk together, *because I was with you.*

5. But now I go my way to him that *originally* sent me. And none of you *need* asketh me, Whither goest thou?

6. But because I have said these things unto you, sorrow hath filled your heart.

7. Nevertheless I tell you the truth, It is expedient for you that I go away. For if I go not away, the *other* Comforter will not come unto you. But if I depart, I will send him unto you *directly*.

8. And when he is come, he will reprove the world of sin, and of righteousness, and of judgment.

9. Of sin, because they *have chosen to* believe not on me.

10. Of righteousness, because I go *unto my Heavenly* Father, and ye see me no more.

11. Of judgment, because the prince of this world is *finally going to be* judged.

12. I have yet many things to say, *and spiritual realities to teach* unto you, but ye cannot bear them now.

13. Howbeit when he, the Spirit of Truth, is come, he will *faithfully* guide you into all truth. For he shall not speak of himself, but whatsoever he shall hear *from the Word of God*, that shall he speak. And he will show you things to come.

14. He shall glorify me. For he shall receive of *that which is* mine, and shall show it unto you.

15. All things that the *Heavenly* Father hath are mine. Therefore said I, that he shall take of *that which is* mine, and shall show it unto you.

16. *A little while* longer, *and ye shall not see me. And again, a little while* longer after that, *and ye shall see me, because I* am going to *go to the* Heavenly *Father.*

17. *Then said some of his disciples among themselves, What is this that he saith unto us, A little while, and ye shall see me; and, Because I go unto the* Heavenly *Father?*

18. *They said therefore, What is this that he saith, A little while? We cannot tell what he saith.*

19. *Now* because of the Holy Spirit gifting of the Word of Knowledge, *Jesus knew that they were desirous to ask him, and said unto them,* Do ye inquire among yourselves of that I said, A little while longer, and ye shall not see me: and again, a little while longer after that, and ye shall see me.

20. *Verily, verily, I say unto you, That ye shall weep and lament, but the world shall* be happy and rejoice. *And ye shall be sorrowful, but your sorrow shall be turned into joy.*

21. *A woman when she is in travail* of birth *hath sorrow, because her hour is come. But as soon as she is delivered of the child, she remembereth no more the anguish, for* the *joy that a man is born into the world.*

22. *And ye now therefore have sorrow* because of my leaving. *But I will see you again, and your heart shall rejoice, and your joy* shall *no man* be able to *taketh from you.*

JOHN 16:23

23. *And in that day ye shall ask me nothing* in prayer. *Verily, verily, I say unto you, Whatsoever ye shall ask the* Heavenly *Father* directly, *in my name, he will give it* unto *you.*

24. *Hitherto have ye asked nothing in* the authority of *my name.* But in that day *ask, and ye shall receive, that your joy may be full.*

25. *These things have I spoken unto you in proverbs. But the time* soon *cometh, when I shall no more speak unto you in proverbs, but I shall show you plainly of the* Heavenly *Father.*

26. *At that day ye shall ask in* the authority of *my name. And I say not unto you, that I will* intercede and pray to *the* Heavenly *Father for you.*

27. *For the* Heavenly *Father himself loveth you, because ye have loved me, and have believed that I came out from God.*

28. *I came forth from* the bosom of *the* Heavenly *Father, and am come into the world* to deal with the Sin problem. *Again, I leave the world, and go un*to the Heavenly *Father.*

29. His disciples said unto him, Lo, now speakest thou plainly, and speakest no proverb.

30. Now are we sure that thou knowest all things, and needest not that any man should ask thee. By this we believe that thou camest forth from God.

31. Jesus answered them, *Do ye now believe?*

32. Behold, the hour cometh, yea, is now come, that ye shall be scattered *like sheep*, every man to his own, *just as the Scripture declares*, and shall leave me alone. And yet I am not alone, because the *Heavenly* Father is *always* with me.

33. These things I have spoken unto you, that in me ye might have a peace *that passes all understanding*. In the world ye shall have tribulation. But be of good cheer, I have overcome the world.

CHAPTER 17

1. These words spake Jesus, and lifted up his eyes to heaven, and said, *Heavenly* Father, the hour is *now* come; glorify thy Son, that thy Son also may glorify thee.

2. As thou hast given him power over all flesh, that he should give Eternal Life to as many as thou hast given *unto* him.

3. And this is *what* Life Eternal *is all about*; that they might *personally* know thee the only True God, and *that they might know* Jesus Christ, whom thou hast sent.

4. I have glorified thee on the earth. I have finished the work which thou gavest me to do.

5. And now, O *Heavenly* Father, glorify thou me *once again* with thine own self, with the glory which I *once* had with thee before the world *ever* was.

JOHN 17:6

6. *I have manifested thy name unto the* Covenant *men which thou gavest* unto *me out of the world. Thine they were* because of the Covenant*, and thou gavest them* unto *me* by thy Spirit*; and they have kept thy word* by choice.

7. *Now they have known that all things whatsoever thou hast given* unto *me are of thee.*

8. *For I have given unto them the words which thou gavest* unto *me. And they have received them* into their heart*, and have known surely that I came out from thee, and they have believed that thou didst send me.*

9. *I pray* and intercede *for them. I pray not for the world* which is not in Covenant with thee*, but for them which thou hast given* unto *me; for they are* Covenantially *thine.*

10. *And all* of *mine are thine, and* all of *thine are mine. And I am glorified in them.*

11. *And now I am no more* going to be *in the world, but these are* still *in the world, and I come* unto thee. *Holy* Heavenly *Father, keep through thine own name,* I pray thee, *those whom thou hast given* unto *me, that they may be one, as we are* one.

12. *While I was with them in the world, I kept them* safe *in thy name. Those that thou gavest* unto *me I have kept. And none of them is lost but,* Judas Iscariot, *the son of perdition; that the Scripture* within the Book of Psalms *might be fulfilled.* (Psalms 109:6-15)

13. *And now come I* unto *thee. And these things I speak in the world, that they might have my joy fulfilled in themselves.*

JOHN 17:25

14. *I have given them thy word. And the world hath hated them, because they are not of the world, even as I am not of the world.*

15. *I pray not that thou shouldest take them out of the world, but that thou shouldest keep them from the evil* that is in the world.

16. *They are not of the world, even as I am not of the world.*

17. *Sanctify* and set *them* apart *through thy truth: thy word is Truth.*

18. *As thou hast sent me into the world, even so have I also sent them into the world.*

19. *And for their sakes I* choose *to sanctify myself, that they also might be sanctified through the Truth* of your word.

20. *Neither pray I for these alone, but for* all of *them also which shall believe on me through their word.*

21. *That they all may be one. As thou,* O Heavenly *Father, art in me, and I* am *in thee, that they also may be one* with*in us. That the world may* then *believe that thou hast sent me.*

22. *And the glory which thou gavest* unto *me I have given* unto *them. That they may be* truly *one, even as we are one.*

23. *I in them, and thou in me, that they may be made perfect* and mature *in one. And that the world may* then *know that thou hast sent me, and hast loved them,* just as much *as thou hast loved me.*

24. *Heavenly* **Father, I will that they also, whom thou hast given** *unto* **me, be with me wherever I am. That they may behold my glory, which thou hast given** *unto* **me. For thou lovedst me** *even* **before the foundation of the world.**

25. **O righteous Father, the world hath not known thee. But I have known thee, and these have known that thou hast sent me.**

26. **And I have declared unto them thy name, and will declare it. That the love wherewith thou hast loved me may be in them, and** *that* **I** *may be* **in them.**

CHAPTER 18

1. **When Jesus had spoken these words, he went forth** *from where he had eaten the Last Supper,* **with his disciples over the brook Cedron, where** *there* **was a garden, into the which he entered, and his disciples** *with him.*

2. **And Judas** *Iscariot* **also, which betrayed him, knew** *of* **the place. For Jesus oftentimes resorted thither with his disciples** *when he was in Jerusalem.*

3. **Judas** *Iscariot* **then, having received a** *temple* **band of men and officers from the chief priests and Pharisees, cometh thither** *to the garden* **with lanterns and torches and weapons.**

4. **Jesus therefore, knowing** *by declaration of the Word of God and the Holy Spirit gifting of the Word of Knowledge* **all things that should come upon him, went forth, and said unto them,** *Whom seek ye?*

5.   They answered him, Jesus of Nazareth. Jesus saith unto them, *I Am.*
6.   As soon then as he had said unto them, *I Am*, they went backward, and fell to the ground.
7.   Then asked he then again, *Whom seek ye?* And they said, Jesus of Nazareth.
8.   Jesus answered, *I have told you that I Am. If therefore ye seek me, let these go their way.*
9.   That the saying might be fulfilled, which he spake, "Of them which thou gavest me have I lost none save the son of perdition." (John 17:12)
10.   Then Simon Peter having a sword drew it, and smote the high priest's servant, and cut off his right ear. The servant's name was Malchus.
11.   Then said Jesus unto Peter, *Put up thy sword into the sheath. The cup which my Heavenly Father hath given me, shall I not drink of it?*
12.   Then the temple band and the captain and officers of the Jews took Jesus, and bound him.
13.   And led him away to Annas first. For he was the former High Priest, and father-in-law to Caiaphas, which was the current High Priest that same year.
14.   Now Caiaphas was he, which prophetically gave counsel unto the Jews, that it was expedient that one man should die for the people rather than that the whole nation should perish. (John 11:50)
15.   And Simon Peter followed Jesus, and so did another disciple called John the Beloved. That disciple was known unto the High Priest, and went in along with Jesus into the palace of the High Priest.

JOHN 18:16

16.   But Peter stood at the door without. Then went out that other disciple *named John* which was known unto the High Priest, and spake unto her that kept the door, and *he* brought in Peter *to the courtyard.*

17.   Then saith the damsel that kept the door unto Peter *as he passed*, Art not thou also one of this man's disciples? *And* he saith, I am not. *And he denied Jesus for the first time.*

18.   And the *palace* servants and officers stood there *within the courtyard*, who had made a fire of coals, for it was cold. And they warmed themselves, and Peter stood with them, and warmed himself.

19.   The *former* High Priest *named Annas* then asked Jesus of his disciples, and of his doctrine.

20.   Jesus answered *unto* him, I spake openly *unto the world. I ever taught in the synagogue, and in the temple, whither the Jews always resort, and in secret have I said nothing.*

21.   *Why askest thou me? Ask them which heard me, what I have said unto them. Behold, they know what I said.*

22.   And when he had thus spoken, one of the *palace* officers which stood by struck Jesus with the palm of his hand, saying, Answerest thou the High Priest so?

23.   Jesus answered him, *If I have spoken evil of the man, bear witness of the evil. But if* I *have spoken well, why smitest thou me?*

24.   Now Annas *after he* had *questioned Jesus,* sent him bound unto Caiaphas the High Priest.

25. And Simon Peter stood and warmed himself *in the courtyard*. They said therefore unto him, Art not thou also one of his disciples? He denied it *a second time*, and said, I am not.

26. One of the servants of the High Priest, being his kinsman whose ear Peter cut off, saith, Did not I *just* see thee in the garden with him?

27. Peter then denied Jesus again *for the third time*. And immediately the cock crew.

28. Then led they Jesus *away* from Caiaphas and unto the Hall of Judgment. And it was *very early in the morning*, and they themselves went not into the Judgment Hall, lest they should become defiled. But *this they did* that they might *be able to* eat the Passover lamb.

29. *Pontius* Pilate then went out *of the Hall of Judgment* unto them, and said, What accusation bring ye against this man?

30. They answered and said unto him, If he were not a malefactor, we would not have delivered him up unto thee.

31. Then said *Pontius* Pilate unto them, Take ye him, and judge him according to your *Mosaic* Law. The *wicked* Jews therefore *lied and* said unto him, It is not lawful for us to put any man to death.

32. That the saying of Jesus might be fulfilled, *of* which he spake, signifying what *kind of a* death he should die.

33. Then *Pontius* Pilate entered into the Judgment Hall again, and called Jesus, and said unto him, Art thou the King of the Jews?

34. **Jesus answered him,** *Sayest thou this thing of thyself, or did others tell it thee of me?*
35. *Pontius* **Pilate answered** *him,* **Am I a Jew? Thine own nation and the** *temple* **chief priests have delivered thee unto me. What hast thou done?**
36. **Jesus answered,** *My kingdom is not of this world. If my kingdom were of this world, then would my servants fight, that I should not be delivered to the Jews. But now is my kingdom not from hence.*
37. *Pontius* **Pilate therefore said unto him, Art thou** *really* **a king then? Jesus answered,** *Thou sayest that I am a king. To this end was I born, and for this cause came I into the world, that I should bear witness unto the Truth. Every one that is of the truth heareth my voice.*
38. *Pontius* **Pilate saith unto him, What is truth? And when he had said this, he went out** *of the Hall of Judgment* **again unto the Jews, and saith unto them, I find in him no fault at all.**
39. **But ye have a custom, that I should release unto you one at the Passover** *Celebration.* **Will ye therefore that I** *should* **release unto you** *Jesus,* **the King of the Jews?**
40. **Then cried they all again, saying,** *Do* **not** *release* **this man** *unto us,* **but Barabbas. Now Barabbas was a robber** *and a murderer.*

CHAPTER 19

1. Then *Pontius* **Pilate therefore took Jesus, and scourged him** *to try and placate the Jews.*
2. **And** *after the scourging,* **the soldiers plaited a crown of thorns, and put it on***to* **his head, and they also put on him a purple robe.**
3. **And said, Hail,** *to the* **King of the Jews! And they smote him with their hands.**
4. *Pontius* **Pilate therefore went forth again, and saith unto them, Behold, I bring him forth** *unto* **you, that ye may know that I find no fault in him.**
5. **Then came Jesus forth, wearing the crown of thorns, and the purple robe. And** *Pontius* **Pilate saith unto them, Behold the man!**
6. **When the chief priests therefore and officers saw him, they cried out saying, Crucify him, crucify him.** *Pontius* **Pilate saith unto them, take ye him** *yourselves,* **and crucify him: for I find no fault in him.**
7. **The Jews answered him, We have a law** *from God,* **and by our law he ought to die, because he made himself** *to be* **the Son of God.**
8. **When** *Pontius* **Pilate therefore heard that saying, he was the more afraid.**
9. **And** *he* **went again unto the Judgment Hall, and saith unto Jesus, Whence art thou** *from?* **But Jesus gave him no answer.**
10. **Then saith** *Pontius* **Pilate unto him, Speakest thou not unto me? Knowest thou not that I have the power to crucify thee, and I have** *the* **power to release thee?**

11. *Jesus answered, Thou couldest have no power at all against me, except it were given unto thee from above. Therefore he that delivered me unto thee hath the greater sin.*
12. And from thenceforth Pontius **Pilate sought to release him. But the Jews cried out, saying, If thou let this man go, thou art not Caesar's friend. Whosoever maketh himself a king speakest against Caesar.**
13. **When** Pontius **Pilate therefore heard that saying, he brought Jesus forth** from the Judgment Hall, **and sat down in the Judgment Seat in a place that is called The Pavement, but in the Hebrew** tongue, **Gabbatha.**
14. **And it was the Preparation** Day **of the Passover** Celebration, **and about the sixth hour. And he saith unto the Jews, Behold your King!**
15. **But they cried out, Away with him! Away with him! Crucify him!** Pontius **Pilate saith unto them, Shall I crucify your King? The chief priests answered, We have no king but Caesar.**
16. **Then delivered he him therefore unto them to be crucified. And they took Jesus, and led him away.**
17. **And he bearing his cross went forth into a place called the place of a skull, which is called in the Hebrew** tongue, **Golgotha**
18. And there is **where they crucified him, and two others with him, on either side one, and Jesus** was **in the midst.**

JOHN 19:25

19. And Pontius **Pilate wrote a title** *on a plaque***, and put it on the cross. And the writing** *of it* **was, JESUS OF NAZARETH THE KING OF THE JEWS.**
20. **This title then read many of the Jews** *within the city*. **For the place where Jesus was crucified was nigh** *unto* **the city. And it was written in** *the* **Hebrew** *tongue***, and** *in* **Greek, and** *in* **Latin.**
21. **Then said the** *temple* **chief priests of the Jews to** *Pontius* **Pilate, Write not, THE KING OF THE JEWS; but that he said, I am King of the Jews.**
22. *Pontius* **Pilate answered, What I have written** *is what* **I have written.**
23. **Then the soldiers, when they had crucified Jesus, took his garments, and made four parts, to every soldier a part. And** *they took* **also his coat. Now the coat was without** *any* **seam, woven from the top throughout.**
24. **They said therefore among themselves, Let us not rend it, but cast lots for it, whose it shall be. So that the Scripture might be fulfilled, which saith, "They parted my raiment among them, and for my vesture they did cast lots."** *(Psalms 22:18)*
25. **Now there stood by the cross of Jesus** *Miriam* **his mother,** *also called Mary*. **And his mother's sister** *named Maria, who was also called Mary*. *As well as* **Mary the wife of Cleophas** *who was a follower of Jesus***, and Mary Magdalene** *out of whom he had cast seven devils*.

26. **When Jesus therefore saw his mother, and the disciple** named John **standing by, whom he loved,** with presence of mind **he saith unto his mother, Woman, behold thy son!**
27. **Then saith he to the disciple, Behold thy mother! And from that hour that disciple took** charge of **her** and led her **unto his own home.**
28. **After this, Jesus knowing** by the Holy Spirit gifting of the Word of Knowledge **that all things were now accomplished,** so that the fullness of the pre-crucifixion Scripture might be fulfilled, **saith, I thirst.**
29. **Now there was set a vessel full of vinegar. And they filled a sponge with vinegar, and put it upon hyssop, and put it to his mouth.**
30. **When Jesus therefore had received the vinegar, he said, It is finished!** Referring to all of the things that needed to be accomplished before his death. **And he bowed his head, and** willingly **gave up the ghost.**
31. **The** ardent **Jews therefore, because it was the Preparation** Day**, that the** dead **bodies should not remain upon the cross on the Sabbath Day, (for that Sabbath Day was an High** Sabbath **Day,) besought** Pontius **Pilate that their legs might be broken** to hasten their death**, and that they might be taken away.**
32. **Then came the soldiers, and brake the legs of the first** malefactor named Gesmis**, and of the other which was crucified with him** named Dismis**.**
33. **But when they came to Jesus, and saw that he was dead already, they** were surprised, and **brake not his legs.**

34. *But one of the soldiers with a spear pierced his side, and forthwith came there out blood and water.*

35. *And he that saw it* was named John, *and he* **bare record, and his record is true. And he knoweth that he saith true, that ye might believe.**

36. *For these things were done, that the Scripture should be fulfilled. "A bone of him shall not be broken."* (Exodus 12:46; Numbers 9:12; Psalms 34:20)

37. *And again another Scripture saith, "They shall look on him whom they pierced."* (Psalms 22:16; Zechariah 12:10)

38. *And after this Joseph of Arimathea, being a disciple of Jesus, but secretly for fear of the Jews, besought* Pontius *Pilate that he might take away the* dead *body of Jesus. And* Pontius *Pilate gave him leave. He came therefore* personally with servants, **and took the** dead **body of Jesus** away.

39. *And there came also* **Nicodemus** to the crucifixion site, *which at the first came to Jesus by night, and* he *brought a mixture of Myrrh and aloes,* of *about a hundred pound weight.*

40. *Then took they the* dead *body of Jesus, and wound it in linen clothes with the spices, as the manner of the Jews is to bury.*

41. *Now in the place where he was crucified there was a garden* which belonged to a rich man. *And in the garden* there was *a new sepulchre, wherein was never* a *man yet laid.*

42. *There laid they Jesus'* dead body *therefore because of the Jews' Preparation Day* and the lateness of the hour. *For the sepulchre was nigh at hand.*

CHAPTER 20

1. ***The first day of the week,*** *which was Sunday,* ***cometh Mary Magdalene early, when it was yet dark,*** *to meet with the other women, so that they might give Jesus a burial fitting for a Prophet of God. And they came* ***unto the sepulchre, and seeth the stone*** *already* ***taken away from the sepulchre.***
2. ***Then she runneth, and cometh to Simon Peter, and to the other disciple*** *named John,* ***whom Jesus loved,*** *who were staying at the house of Cleophas while they were in Jerusalem.* ***And*** *she* ***saith unto them, They have taken away the Lord out of the sepulchre, and we know not where they have laid him.***
3. ***Peter therefore*** *hurriedly* ***went forth, and that other disciple, and*** *they* ***came*** *unto* ***the sepulchre.***
4. ***So they ran both together. And the other disciple****, being younger,* ***did outrun Peter, and came first to the sepulchre.***
5. ***And he stooping down, and looking in, saw the linen clothes lying*** *there.* ***Yet went he not in.***
6. ***Then cometh Simon Peter following*** *after* ***him, and*** *he* ***went*** *right* ***into the sepulchre, and*** *also* ***seeth the linen clothes lie,***
7. ***And the napkin, that was*** *wound* ***about his head, not lying with the linen clothes, but wrapped together in a place by itself.***
8. ***Then went in also that other disciple*** *named John,* ***which came first to the sepulchre, and he saw, and*** *he* ***believed*** *that something wonderful had happened.*

9. *For as yet they knew not the Scripture, that he must rise again from the dead.* (Psalms 16:10-11)

10. *Then the disciples went away again* back *unto their own home* with Cleophas.

11. *But Mary* being winded by all of the running, **stood without at the sepulchre weeping. And as she wept, she stooped down into the sepulchre** once again, and stood facing the place where the body had been.

12. *And* for the second time she **seeth two angels in white sitting, the one at the head, and the other at the feet,** of where the dead **body of Jesus had lain.**

13. *And they say unto her, Woman, why weepest thou? She saith unto them* through her tears, *Because they have taken away my Lord, and I know not where they have laid him.*

14. *And when she had thus said*, and purposed to compose herself, **she turned herself** back for the first time, toward the sepulchre entrance, **and saw Jesus standing** in the entrance, **and knew not that it was Jesus** because he was backlit from the rising sun.

15. *Jesus saith unto her,* *Woman, why weepest thou? Whom seekest thou?* *She, supposing him to be the gardener* because of the early hour of the day, **saith unto him, Sir, if thou have borne him hence, tell me where thou hast laid him, and I will** come and **take him away.** As she spoke, Mary turned herself for the second time, and gestured back to where the body had once lain.

JOHN 20:16

16.   *Jesus saith unto her,* Mary. **She** *suddenly recognizing the sweetness of his voice,* **turned herself** *for the third time,* **and** *extending her arms to embrace him* **saith unto him, Rabboni: which is to say, Master!**

17.   *Jesus saith unto her,* Touch me not! For I am not yet ascended to my Heavenly Father. But go unto my brethren, and say unto them, I ascend unto my Heavenly Father, and to your Heavenly Father, and to my God and to your God.

18.   **Mary Magdalene** *then* **came and told the disciples that she had seen the Lord, and that he had spoken these things unto her.** *But they believed her not.*

19.   **Then the same** *Sun***day at evening, being the first day of the week, when the doors were shut** *and locked* **where the disciples were assembled for fear of the** *murderous* **Jews, came Jesus and stood in the midst** *of the eleven, which included Judas Iscariot,* **and saith unto them,** Peace be unto you.

20.   **And when he had so said, he showed unto them** *the piercing of* **his hands and his side. Then were the disciples glad, when they saw the Lord.**

21.   **Then said Jesus** *un***to them again,** Peace be unto you. As my Father hath sent me *forth,* even so send I you.

22.   **And when he had said this, he breathed on them, and saith unto them,** Receive ye the Holy Ghost. *And as he exhaled, they were all Born-Again within their spirit at that very moment, including Judas Iscariot.*

23.   *Then said Jesus unto them,* Whosesoever sins ye remit, they are remitted unto them, and whosesoever sins ye retain, they are retained.

JOHN 20:31

24. But *doubting* **Thomas,** *who was* **one of the twelve, called Didymus, was not with them when Jesus came** *on that Sunday evening.*

25. **The other disciples therefore said unto him** *when they were together,* **We have seen the Lord. But he said unto them, Except I shall see in his hands the print of the nails** *for myself,* **and put my finger into the print of the nails, and thrust my hand into his side, I will not believe.**

26. **And after eight** *more* **days** *had passed,* **again his disciples were within** *the room,* **and Thomas** *was* **with them. Then came Jesus, the doors being shut** *and locked,* **and stood in the midst, and said,** Peace be unto you.

27. **Then saith he to Thomas,** Reach hither thy finger, and behold my hands. And reach hither thy hand, and thrust it into my side. And be not faithless, but believing.

28. **And Thomas answered and said unto him, My Lord and my God.**

29. **Jesus saith unto him,** Thomas, because thou hast seen me, thou hast believed. Blessed are they that have not seen *me,* and yet have believed.

30. **And many other signs truly did Jesus in the presence of his disciples, which are not written** *with***in this book.**

31. **But these** *things* **are written, that ye might believe that Jesus** *of Nazareth* **is the Christ, the** *Only Begotten* **Son of God. And that** *in* **believing ye might have Life though his name.**

CHAPTER 21

1. **After these things** had passed, **Jesus showed himself again to the disciples at the Sea of Tiberias. And on this wise showed he himself.**
2. **There were together Simon Peter, and Thomas called Didymus, and Nathanael of Cana in Galilee, and** James and John **the sons of Zebedee, and two other of his disciples.**
3. **Simon Peter saith unto them, I go a fishing. They say unto him, We** will **also go with thee. They went forth, and entered into a ship immediately, and that night they caught nothing.**
4. **But when the morning was now come, Jesus stood on the shore. But the disciples knew not that it was Jesus.**
5. **Then Jesus saith unto them,** Children, have ye any meat? **They answered** unto **him, No.**
6. **And he said unto them,** by virtue of the Holy Spirit gifting of the Word of Knowledge, Cast the net on the right side of the ship, and ye shall find. **They cast therefore, and now they were not able to draw it** in **for the multitude of fishes** that were in the net.
7. **Therefore that disciple whom Jesus loved** named John, **saith unto Peter, It is the Lord!**
8. **And** one of **the other disciples came in a little ship, (for they were not far from** the **land, but as it were two hundred cubits,) dragging the net with** the **fishes** in it.

9.   As soon then as they were come to *the* **land, they saw a fire of coals** *burning* **there, and** *there were* **fish laid thereon, and** *some* **bread.**

10.   **Jesus saith unto them,** *Bring of the fish which ye have now caught.*

11.   **Simon Peter went up** *to the small boat*, **and drew the net to** *the* **land** *which was* **full of great fishes, a hundred and fifty and three. And for all** *that* **there were**, *being* **so many, yet was not the net broken.**

12.   **Jesus saith unto them,** *Come and dine.* **And none of the disciples durst ask him, Who art thou? Knowing that it was the Lord.**

13.   **Jesus then cometh, and taketh** *of the* **bread, and giveth** *it unto* **them, and** *the* **fish likewise.**

14.   **This is now the third time that Jesus showed himself to his disciples, after that he was risen from the dead.**

15.   **So when they had dined, Jesus saith** *unto* **Simon Peter,** *Simon, son of Jonas, lovest thou me more than* thou lovest *these?* **He saith unto him, Yea, Lord; thou knowest that I love thee. He saith unto him,** *Feed my lambs.*

16.   **He saith to him again the second time,** *Simon, son of Jonas, lovest thou me?* **He saith unto him, Yea, Lord; thou knowest that I love thee. He saith unto him** *Feed my sheep.*

17.   **He saith unto him the third time,** *Simon, son of Jonas, lovest thou me?* **Peter was grieved because he** *had* **said unto him the third time, Lovest thou me? And he said unto him, Lord thou knowest all things. Thou knowest that I love thee. Jesus saith unto him,** *Feed my sheep.*

JOHN 21:18

18. *Verily, verily, I say unto thee, When thou wast young, thou girdest thyself, and walkedst whither thou wouldest. But when thou shalt be old, thou shalt stretch forth thy hands, and another shall gird thee, and carry thee whither thou wouldest not.*

19. **This spake he, signifying by what death he should** *ultimately* **glorify God. And when he had** *thus* **spoken this, he saith unto him,** *Follow me.*

20. **Then Peter, turning** *himself* **about, seeth the disciple whom Jesus loved following. Which** *was he* **also** *who* **leaned on his breast at** *the* **Last Supper, and** *who* **said** *unto the* **Lord, Which is he that betrayeth thee?**

21. **Peter seeing him saith** *unto* **Jesus, Lord, and what shall this man do?**

22. **Jesus saith unto him,** *If I should will that he tarry until I come again, what is that to thee? Follow thou me.*

23. **Then went this saying abroad** *as a rumor* **among the brethren, that that disciple should not die. Yet Jesus said not unto him** *that***, He shall not die. But,** *If I should will that he tarry until I come again, what is that to thee?*

24. **This is the** *very* **disciple which testifieth of these things, and** *he* **wrote these things. And we know** *of a certainty* **that his testimony is true.** *And shortly after these things, because of a lack of protective prayer covering from Jesus, Judas Iscariot became swallowed-up by the Spirit of Heaviness, and he went out and hanged himself.*

25. *And there are also many other things which Jesus did, the which, if they should* all *be written* down *every one, I suppose that even the world itself could not contain the* number of *books that should be written. Amen.*

Meet the Author

By-The-Book Ministries, Inc. began in 2001 as a teaching outreach. Rob E. Daley has been gifted by God to be able to explain biblical truths in an easy to understand manner.

Many have been blessed by his teaching style.

Rob was saved and filled with the Holy Spirit in 1978 and has been instructed by the greatest teacher of all—the Spirit of Truth Himself. Rob is an ordained minister with the Assemblies of God International Fellowship and has pastored in various churches over the past 34 years.

It is the desire of this ministry to see the body of Christ solidly taught, and grow up into the things of the Lord. Rob is available for seminars, retreats, conventions, etc.

Rob can be reached at:

thedaleys@bythebookministries.org

http://robdaleyauthor.com

www.ingramcontent.com/pod-product-compliance
Lightning Source LLC
Chambersburg PA
CBHW042337150426
43195CB00001B/22